BENEATH A HERETIC'S WINGS.

Carlton Pearson, Apostasy,
and the Evangelical Establishment

BENEATH A HERETIC'S WINGS:

Carlton Pearson, Apostasy, and the Evangelical Establishment

Cassandra L. McClellan & Teresa L. Reed

GarySprings
Independent Press, LLC
Tulsa, Oklahoma

BENEATH A HERETIC'S WINGS

Published by GarySprings Independent Press, LLC, Tulsa, OK.

Copy Edited by Brooklyn Symone Russell, Merrillville, IN.

Designed by Terralyn Roach, TSR Creative, Louisville, KY.

Cover by D'mitri Sobol, Valor Biz Professional Services, Raleigh, NC.

Back cover design by Terralyn Roach, TSR Creative, Louisville, KY.

Back cover photos by Colin Bent, Colin Bent Photography, Broken Arrow, OK.

Scriptures quoted are from the King James Version (KJV) Bible, unless otherwise noted.

ISBN: 978-0-578-40156-0

Dedication

*We dedicate this book to two brothers, one in Heaven,
the other still with us on Earth.*

Pastor Jesse L. Williams, your light ever radiates from beyond the clouds, and the powerful life you lived still shines in our memories.

Pastor David B. Smith, your rock-solid dedication and consistency have given us comfort and hope. Both your integrity and your music sound in our hearts in more ways than you can possibly know.

May all who read these words be inspired by the examples
of Christ that you each represent.

✝

*"I alone cannot change the world, but
I can cast a stone across the water
to create many ripples."*

-Mother Teresa

CONTENTS

Chronology ix

Preface xiii

Chapter 1:   *Prophecy* 1

Chapter 2:   *You could feel it. That fire, that electricity* 9

Chapter 3:   *It was in the back, right next to a pole* 27

Chapter 4:   *...that glorious week in April of Heaven
              on Earth* 45

Chapter 5:   *I'd come a long way from my
              safe and inconspicuous place* 59

Chapter 6:   *The air stood still* 69

Chapter 7:   *There was a restlessness that drove Bishop Pearson* 85

Chapter 8:   *The exodus from Higher D began as a trickle* 91

Chapter 9:   *In every empty seat, I saw the person who
              was once there* 115

Chapter 10:   *I wanted to share my healing with others*....................123

Chapter 11:   *We still had a mortgage and utilities to pay* 147

Chapter 12:   *But he was my friend. But he was gay* 157

Chapter 13:   *We barely broke even, and time was running out* 163

Chapter 14:   *It was Christmas Day, 2005* 177

Chapter 15:   *The feature, titled "Heretic," aired on
              December 16, 2005* 181

Chapter 16: *All of the remarks came from church-going people* 191

Chapter 17: *He was suffering from exhaustion, maybe* 199

Chapter 18: *Our normal was no longer the same* 205

Chapter 19: *We were terminally ill. We would die.*
The sense of uncertainty took its toll 211

Chapter 20: *And then, in the wee hours, the phone rang* 219

Chapter 21: *The commitment at All Souls is to love*
beyond belief 223

Chapter 22: *I recalled what Bishop Veron Ashe said* 227

Chapter 23: *That seat, in that place, at that moment,*
was like pure gold 231

Postlude: Reflections 237

Chronology of the Life and Ministry of Carlton D. Pearson

1953   Carlton D'Metrius Pearson was born to Adam Pearson and Lillie Ruth Johnson Pearson on March 19th in San Diego, California

1968   Licensed to preach at age fifteen by Bishop J.A. Blake

1971   Began study at Oral Roberts University in Tulsa, Oklahoma

1976   Worked for Oral Roberts Evangelistic Association (OREA) as an Associate Evangelist

1977   Founded Higher Dimensions, Inc. (HDI)

1981   Founded Higher Dimensions Evangelistic Center in Jenks, Oklahoma

1983   Higher Dimensions Evangelistic Center moved to 8621 S. Memorial Drive in Tulsa

1988   Hosted the first annual Azusa Conference, Tulsa, Oklahoma

1994   Married Gina Marie Gauthier on September 3rd; Higher Dimensions Evangelistic Center is later renamed Higher Dimensions Family Church

1995   The first *Live at Azusa* album is recorded and released

1995   Pearson shared stage with President Bill Clinton at memorial service following the April 19th Oklahoma City bombing

1995   Pearson's son, Julian D'Metrius, was born on July 9th

1997   Pearson was consecrated to the Bishopric during the Azusa Conference in April

1997   Pearson's daughter, Majeste' Amor, was born on October 29th

1997   *Live at Azusa 2* was recorded and released

1999   *Live at Azusa 3* was recorded and released

2000   Bishop Veron Ashe gave an ominous prophecy on March 26th

2000   Pearson began shift to an inclusive doctrine

2001   *Live at Azusa 4* was recorded and released; Azusa Conference was held at Mabee Center for the last time

2001   Pearson was awarded an honorary doctorate from Christian Life School of Theology

2001   *Tulsa World* newspaper announced Carlton Pearson's run for mayor on October 31st

2002   *Azusa Praise: We Cry Out* was recorded at Azusa Conference at Tulsa Convention Center

2003   Last conference in the tradition of Azusa was held at 8621 S. Memorial Drive

2003   Pearson was denounced as a heretic by the Joint College of African American Pentecostal Bishops

2005   National Public Radio aired, for the first time, the story of Pearson's doctrinal shift in its episode titled "Heretic" on *This American Life* on December 16th

2005   Higher Dimensions held its last service at 8621 S. Memorial Drive on December 31st, with court order to vacate the property by January 1, 2006

2006   Higher Dimensions congregation began worshipping at Trinity Episcopal Church on January 1st; Higher Dimensions was then renamed "New Dimensions"

2006   Pearson completed his book, *The Gospel of Inclusion*; it was not offered in bookstores for another two years

2008   A single Tulsa bookstore, Barnes & Noble, hosted a book signing and offered *The Gospel of Inclusion* for sale for the first time

2008   New Dimensions left Trinity Episcopal and began worshipping at All Souls Unitarian Church in June

2008   The former Higher Dimensions congregation worshipped as an independent body for the last time; the church originally founded by Carlton Pearson in 1981 officially dissolved on August 31st. Some members join with All Souls, where they remain today

2009   Pearson accepted position as interim pastor of Christ Universal Temple in Chicago, Illinois

2015   Pearson returned to Tulsa, Oklahoma

2015   Adam "Dad" Pearson passed away on March 21st

2015   *Charisma Magazine* published the news of divorce filed by Gina Pearson on August 25th

2016   Harvard University acquired Pearson's personal papers for its archive

2018   The feature film *Come Sunday*, which chronicles Bishop Pearson's transformation, premiered at multiple film festivals, at Tulsa's Circle Cinema on April 8th, and on Netflix on April 13th

PREFACE

Religion is like fire; it sustains and it destroys. It comforts and it divides, teaching love perhaps as powerfully as it can trigger hate. In every religion, there is an obscure place somewhere between what is known, what is believed, and what one has been taught to believe. At the dawn of the new millennium, Tulsa, Oklahoma witnessed a crack in a seemingly impenetrable wall of Evangelical dogma, a belief firmly in place at least since the time of St. Augustine.

When an Evangelical superstar dared to question the fifteen-hundred-year-old notion of an eternal hell, the fallout was enormous. It shook the very foundation of Bible-Belt Christianity, and its repercussions were felt around the world. Two women recall being at the epicenter of this spiritual revolution. They remember its hurts and joys, its losses and gains, and the many lessons along the way. They learned of a God whose love transcends the Church.

Teresa Reed is from Gary, Indiana. She is a professor and author, and lives with her husband, James. She first attended Higher Dimensions in the late 1980s and joined in 1994. Cassandra McClellan is from Sand Springs, Oklahoma. She is a mother, grandmother, singer, playwright, and social media coordinator. She works as an international customer service specialist. She came to Higher Dimensions in 1995. Here is their story.

CHAPTER 1

PROPHECY

For thousands of years, humankind has entertained the notion that there are those among us who can see into the future. At times, they are called *psychics*; at other times, *prophets*. They've found a place in popular culture, in late-night infomercials, and on reality TV. Sometimes, their celebrity trappings make it difficult for intelligent people to take them seriously. They often seem like frauds exploiting the emotional vulnerability of gullible people. Yet, the historical record is clear. There are well-documented cases, eerie and uncanny, of people who seem to know things before they happen.

Leonardo DaVinci drew images of a flying machine over four hundred years before the Wright Brothers. Novelist Morgan Robertson wrote about the ill-fated maiden voyage of a large ship colliding with an iceberg fourteen years before the *Titanic*. Edgar Cayce predicted the 1929 stock market crash four years before it occurred. And Archbishop Veron Ashe came to Tulsa, Oklahoma and delivered a prophetic utterance that no one at the time understood.

The various expressions of Christianity can exhibit striking differences. For the more liturgical denominations (Catholics, Lutherans, and Episcopalians, for example), worship is time-honored, scripted, sedate, and well-rehearsed. Words are spoken, prayers are prayed, and music is heard, all in a predictably unfolding sequence that repeats from Sunday to Sunday. Spontaneity, if any, is beautifully contained. Not so in Pentecostal traditions. By contrast, Pentecostals — especially African-American Pentecostals — expect and value spontaneity. They value the wind of the Spirit and gladly go in the direction it blows. The likelihood of hearing a prophetic utterance at a Catholic or Lutheran church is virtually null. But in Pentecostal circles, these are dramatic and valued occurrences that, though rare, can happen at any time.

An odd-looking white man, Veron Ashe was an anomaly. He was born in 1968 into a family of great wealth and spent his childhood in Miami. His earliest background was Catholic. However, the family maid was a black woman of West-Indian origin who exposed Ashe to the spirituality of the black church when he was a child. He later became Orthodox. Along with his Orthodox affiliation, Bishop Ashe was fluent in the style and dialect of black, Pentecostal preaching. Sporting a soup-bowl haircut and wearing the floor-length, regal vestments of the Orthodox Church, his liturgical image stood in stark contrast to the fiery flare of his sermons. He seemed an amalgam, an unusual combination of both the staid and the more spirited elements of Christianity in one human being.[1]

By the 1990s, Ashe had attracted the curiosity and the notice of the Evangelical establishment. On March 26, 2000, Evangelical megastar Carlton Pearson hosted Ashe as a guest speaker at his church, Higher Dimensions, in Tulsa, Oklahoma. During the course of his sermon, a sanctuary of over a thousand curious onlookers listened as Ashe shifted into a mood of solemnity. Clearly, the Holy Spirit had overcome him. Pacing the floor of the chancel, Veron Ashe gave this prophetic utterance (transcribed verbatim):

There are higher dimensions. You will be persecuted because you'll dare to go there. The days that are ahead will be harder than any days you have walked in times past. Hear the Word of the Lord. But what God has prepared for you in the days that are ahead of you will bring more persecution and more tribulation, and more hungry people will identify with your message. And the religious will say, "we told you so." The day will come, says the Lord of Hosts to this house, that people through the nations shall identify with you, and those you called your friends shall deny you. Those that you've discipled and those that you've fathered will say, "I never knew you." And those that you've never met face to face will say, "You have been a father to us without ever seeing us." For this house has always paid a price, this house has never got anything easy. The Lord says, "Other churches I have blessed, I have prospered, but for everything I've done in this place, the Lord says it has cost you. It has cost you people, it has cost you friends, it has cost you those that you loved and those that you've cared for. Now the day is ahead that it shall be even worse, says the Lord of Hosts, for the accusations shall fly and the day shall come that those that have praised you will condemn you and those that cried "Hosanna!" will cry "Crucify!" The articles and the magazines that [wrote] praise for you will begin to question you theologically says the Lord of Hosts; but you shall preach my heart. For the Lord says, I've never called you to fit in the religious circles. I called you to preach to my people. And there are people who have been broken and have nowhere to turn. Bishop, I spoke to you in the beginning says the Lord of Hosts, and the Lord says to this house there are two people that are welcome. There are two people that are always welcome here, says the Lord of Hosts, the hungry and the hurting. So the Lord says, I shall send to this house those that are hungry and those that are hurting. And those that are not hungry and those that are not hurting, I shall remove. For there are some that sit in your pulpit now that will not sit in your pulpit two years from now. There are some that have called you "father" but will deny they ever knew you. There are some that you have mentored, trained, and poured your life into. And the Lord says that they shall deny that you had anything to do with it. Count it not a strange thing, for these are the things you've already counted up, the Lord says, and now is the day that you shall walk them out. Fear not, for you shall not lack in any [food] for the stand that you shall take, for those that have rejected you are the religious, but those who will accept you shall be the secular. The Lord says such a strange thing shall begin to take place. For you shall begin to find doors open even as I have already done, says the Lord of Hosts, but there shall be doors open to this church in strange places, strange television, strange radio, strange things, says the Lord of Hosts. The religious world will separate and distinguish itself, but you shall begin to find my presence in the strangest of places and the strangest of people. The phone shall begin to ring off the hook, says the Lord, with people of renown name who've said, "I've never felt comfortable in anybody's church, but I heard you, and for the first time I feel like I can be accepted for who I am and not what I have." The Lord says to this place, Behold, you ask for it, you get it. You've called yourself "Higher Dimensions." Now the day is coming that I shall bring you to places you could not even begin to perceive. For the Lord says, that this day shall be a unique and strange day, says the Lord of Hosts, there shall come such a mandate upon my manservant, and even his wife, says the Lord of Hosts. There shall be such a strange anointing and such a strange ministry that shall flow through her says the Lord of Hosts that it will not even be perceived, for she has literally been a vessel filled with truth. And there are those who have literally questioned her maturity in the Kingdom and what right does she have to be speaking in conferences but the Lord says her maturity came not because of her spiritual age but because of her openness to my spirit, says the Lord of Hosts. For she was unlearned in the ways of the Church, but learned in the ways of God. The Lord says that there's a word in her that shall deliver many people and shall set many people free. And she shall even make more friends than you by accident, she'll make more friends by accident than you did on purpose. The Lord says literally she shall minister out of her own heart, for she's a woman who can minister the heart of God, the compassion of God, she can love anybody, anywhere, and will meet very famous and important people that shall literally say, "I don't know why, I don't know what it is about you, but there's something about you I just like." God says, he shall give her a voice to the multitudes to heal those that nobody else would want to touch, to heal those that no one else would want to be connected to. So the Lord says to Higher Dimensions, prepare yourselves, for there's a realm in God that you're about to experience, a place that you're about to walk into, a level of God that you're about to see. God says don't fear when the radio reports come, and the television and the Christian magazines, for all of those things, you have already counted the cost, and it shall not be important. For I did not call you to be accepted by the Pharisees. I called you to preach the Gospel to those who would hear. So the Lord says Behold, they're coming. Those that you have prayed for and those that you have cried out for are coming. And when they come, you shall stand in amazement and say, "where did they come from?" For the pagans shall come. The unbelievers shall come. The Muslims shall come. The Jews shall come, the Hindus shall come, and they will come and they will sit and they will not believe immediately, says the Lord, but they will come and they will listen. And they will be touched by the love of God that this house will share. For the days are coming ahead that there shall be unique doors that shall be open. For you shall meet major people in major television networks. And you shall have words for them that will not be necessarily "Thus says the Lord," but they shall be words of friendship and words of healing. And unique things shall begin to take place in this church . . . .".[2]

That particular worship service concluded as it typically did, with the energized and bustling congregation hearing the final benediction. They then erupted into joyful chatter as they began spilling into the crowded parking lot of Higher Dimensions. Some headed to local restaurants, others hugged each other goodbye until the next service. At the time, the prophecy seemed quickly forgotten by most. Life went on as usual.

His vestments were one aspect of his identity, and his Pentecostal fervor, another. Bishop Ashe harbored yet a third aspect of his personality, one that was sad, tragic, and largely unknown. The last months of his life were harrowing and included alcohol addiction and run-ins with the law. According to internet gossip, he was gay. Bishop Ashe died on January 18, 2014, just shy of his 46th birthday.

---

1. Print references to Veron Ashe are relatively sparse. Aces High Studios and Oracle TV News both posted video tributes to Veron Ashe covering his life, ministry, and death. As of this writing, Mar Thomas Orthodox Church also features a tribute to Veron Ashe on its website (https://www.marthomaorthodoxchurch.org/our-leaders).

2. Aces High Studios posted a video of the prophecy referenced here at the following URL: https://www.youtube.com/watch?v=paoUyxRsKw4.

CHAPTER 2

"You could feel it. That fire, that electricity..."

-Teresa

For African Americans, church is the one thing that is constant; it is *always* there. It is there when we are born, when we are baptized, when we marry, and when we bury. Church affirms us in our hopes and cradles us in our sorrows. Its walls vibrate with the soulfulness of our singing and clapping, its floors with the rhythm of our shouting. Church is the sound of spirit and celebration, the smell of fried chicken, pressed hair, and the good, "special occasion" cologne. Church is our sacred go-to space, our portal to other-worldliness. It is the one place where we can express the fullness of our God-loving blackness, where we can be the best of ourselves and the worst of ourselves and still find acceptance. It's where we can safely praise, cry, scream, shout, and be normal doing all of that with others who do the same. For us, Church is as stable as a tree with roots a hundred miles deep, firmly planted by the ever-changing streams of life. Church is mother, father, and family. It is home.

Black churches come in all types and sizes. Some of our churches are little store-fronts with fifteen or twenty members and grandiose names. *Universal World Outreach Miracle Deliverance Center*, for example, uses a building that was once a Dairy Queen and has, at best, seventeen regular members. The windows are the same ones where people once ordered hot fudge sundaes. The cardboard cross on the wall is beside the imprint showing where the custard machine used to be.

Other black churches are imposing structures with stained-glass windows, high ceilings, pipe organs, and well-worn traditions. These churches have red carpet and varnished, knotty pine pews; the hymnals in the wooden pew backs have cracked and yellowing pages and Sunday school fans with popsicle-stick handles and picture-perfect chocolate families. The mother on the fan wears a pink pillbox hat with a little fishnet veil, and the father is dressed in a dark suit with a pencil-thin tie. The little girl wears white, lace gloves and clutches a Bible, while her brother beside her has plump jaws and a very deliberate part in the side of his head. The two-dimensional, cardboard family is the picture of religious perfection. On the reverse side of the Sunday School fan is the address and phone number to Jack's Funeral Home.

Along with the stained glass, the wooden pews, and the Sunday school fans, these churches usually have a fairly large framed picture of Martin Luther King, Jr. in the lobby and baptismal records that go back generations. The cornerstone tells the year that the ground was broken. It was a very long time ago.

Still others are ultra-modern megachurches. Run like corporations, these black churches often have cutting-edge technology and multi-racial crowds numbering in the thousands. Instead of hymnals, they have giant drop-down screens where song lyrics on a PowerPoint file are projected so that congregants can follow along. Fashionable and sophisticated, the black megachurch markets itself and its Gospel message with all the trappings of modernity and the far reach of the Digital Age. These churches are typically upbeat, non-denominational, and economically progressive, even if they are sometimes socially and politically conservative. Pastors TD Jakes, Creflo Dollar, Fred Price, and Noel Jones are celebrity preachers, all millionaires who straddle the fence between piety and prosperity, the sacred and the mainstream. The pastors of these megachurches, while ministers by profession, are often savvy and shameless entrepreneurs with one or more lucrative side hustles.

The black megachurch is usually Evangelical. It takes literally the mandate to go into all of the world and preach the Gospel. Its goal is to expand by winning souls to Jesus Christ. Numbers matter. The more souls won, the more proof that the Gospel is being spread. And often, these churches are Pentecostal, exhibiting the spontaneity of the Spirit.

Before Jakes, Dollar, and Jones, there was a pioneer who came from the unlikeliest of places and settled in the buckle of the Bible Belt. He was a West-Coast native transplanted to Tulsa, Oklahoma, a city both famous for its religious industry and infamous for its racial tension. His name was Carlton Pearson, and his church was Higher Dimensions Evangelistic Center.

In the 1980s, Higher Dimensions cut the archetype and set the bar for the black megachurch. "Higher D," as we affectionately called it, was founded in 1981 in a storefront in nearby Jenks, Oklahoma and quickly grew to number in the thousands. Within a few years, it occupied prime acreage on Tulsa's South Memorial Drive. Its ministries included a food pantry called Raven's Nest, Hannah's Prayer Adoption Agency, a preschool, a home for unwed mothers, a bookstore, a prison ministry, a credit union, a counseling center, a music and dance ministry, the annual Azusa Conference, and the Azusa School of Ministry. That a black pastor was the leader of a multiracial congregation in Tulsa was a source of immense pride for all of us. We never expected it to die.

Fast forward to the late 1990s, and to a typical Sunday morning during the heyday of Higher D. To accommodate the large crowds, there were three Sunday services. Sunday mornings started with an early service which began at 8:30. Its attendees were mostly white people and former Catholics accustomed to abbreviated worship that started and finished promptly. The main service started at 11:00am and was for everyone else, those who didn't mind lingering a while and finishing by around 1pm, as the Spirit led. A third service was in the evening. Although the official start time of the main morning service was 11:00, everyone knew that to arrive after 10:45am was to have little luck of finding a parking space, and even less of a chance of getting a seat in the sanctuary. By 10:30, South Memorial Drive was already clogged with anxious traffic and holy road-rage, Christians dressed "to the Nines" and frantic to claim their favorite seat on their favorite row at Higher Dimensions.

As members of the sixty-voice choir, we were required to arrive early and be present for both services. In preparation for the main service we were to be seated in our places by 10:30. Like most members of Higher D, we came from more traditional churches, from different parts of the country, where the rules for choir membership were very relaxed and informal. Most of us grew up in churches that allowed anybody to join the choir, regardless of how tone-deaf or off-key they were. We referenced the scripture in Psalms that calls on "everything that has breath" to praise the Lord, our way of excusing singers whose skills failed to match their aspirations. As a child, I sat respectfully as many well-meaning church members butchered our beloved hymns with their lack of vocal ability. Not at Higher D. Every choir member had to pass an audition and attend six weeks of mandatory rehearsal before graduating to sing in the Sunday morning service. Many sincere aspirants who auditioned simply didn't make the cut. Even though I had a degree in Music, I remember my own audition for the Higher D Choir. I felt like a contestant on *Showtime at the Apollo*; trembling with fear and intimidated by those already initiated, I used all my courage to perform my audition piece as the veteran members sized me up. Membership in the Higher D Choir was not a right; it was a hard-won privilege. And when we sang, the rafters moved.

From our elevated vantage point at the front of the sanctuary behind the altar, we could see it all: The greeters stationed at each door, wearing their name badges, smiling warmly and handing out programs to those who entered; the ushers dressed in their starched white blouses and black skirts, extending their white-gloved hands, policing the crowd in the name of Jesus and directing foot traffic; people leaving their Bibles and purses to claim the seats where they would return after a quick visit to the restroom or the bookstore; friends embracing each other heartily as though they hadn't just seen each other a few days earlier at Wednesday-night Bible Study; parents warning their kids to behave before they rushed them off to the highly popular and well-structured Children's Church in another part of the building. By 10:50, the first ten rows in the sanctuary were already filled, and in the minutes following, the rows behind them were quickly filling too, like a sold-out stadium at the Super Bowl.

Across from the choir stand, the bass guitarist strapped on his instrument and the drummer took his place, carefully choosing his pair of sticks and trying out the snare and the foot pedal. As he tightened his snare, the lead guitarist checked his amplifier. The Hammond B-3 organ was warmed and ready. David Smith played an elaborate chord, and the pianist at the Steinway a few feet away echoed it back. Anticipation was building. The other musicians tuned up, organ playing another riff, piano answering back, lead guitar playing another riff . . . BAM, the Spirit was already there! Still a few minutes till 11:00, but the Spirit was already there. You could feel it. That fire, that electricity – already there.

The Church Mothers, dressed in their finest and crowned in their majestic, colorful Sunday-go-to-meeting hats, were all in their places. They gradually ceased their greetings and conversations and begin to mutter under their breath the name of Jesus, checking things in the spirit realm. A few of the Prayer Warriors paced the altar back and forth, speaking in tongues, stirring the atmosphere, welcoming the Spirit, already present, already working. Their facial expressions took on a devout severity because it was nearly time. The excited chatter of Church Family reunited again was overtaken by a holy hush. The Fire. The Anointing. The Electricity. The Anticipation. God was already in the room.

Now, every parking space was filled. The closest spaces were now blocks away. From balcony to floor, every seat in the auditorium was claimed. Standing room only. By order of the Fire Marshall, the place was at capacity and no one else could enter. Late waking up? Too bad. Slow getting dressed?

You've missed out. Once you had that seat, you dare not move. That seat, in that place, at that moment, was worth gold. You dare not move.

And then, at the stroke of 11:00, the Praise Leader, Brenda Todd, bounded toward the pulpit like an Olympian.[1] She was a stunningly beautiful woman. Her chocolate brown skin was flawless, and her makeup was star-quality and camera-ready. Her shiny, jet-black hair was coiffed in an immaculate up-do, and she wore a flowing outfit with metallic-gold accents and jewelry and shoes to match. Though sufficiently elegant to belong on the cover of a magazine, this woman was a fearsome Commando.

With supernatural energy, Brenda Todd grabbed the microphone, and addressed the congregation, calling the service to order in her powerful, rich, sing-song tenor voice: "Are you all ready to stand up and give God some PRAAAAAAAIIIIIIISEEEEE!!" In an instant, thousands of us were to our feet – young and old, black, white, Latino, Native American, rich and poor, educated and blue-collar workers, former Catholics, former Baptists, former Methodists–anxious, excited and thirsty people, eager to feel God.

Immediately, we were transported. The music was on fire – organ, drums, bass, lead guitar, and screaming saxophone in conversation with a colorful, multi-ethnic sea of swaying bodies, clapping hands, and arms raised. The whole of us felt moved and lifted by an unseen force, our demographic differences dissolved by what we called the Anointing.

Brenda Todd led the congregation through a medley of rousing praise songs. At the height of our celebration, the core pastoral staff and church leaders—about a dozen of them—entered from the back of the sanctuary and came down the center aisle to take their designated places on the elevated pulpit. The processional of ministers was an indication of Higher D's size and complexity. There was an Assistant Pastor, a Youth Pastor, a Children's Pastor, a Pastor over Music and Fine Arts, a Pastor over Operations, a Pastor over Finance, a Pastor over the Counseling Center, and a host of other directors and leaders of various church entities. Every Sunday morning, this contingent of church leadership – itself racially integrated – entered singing and praising like the rest of us. At the very end of the processional was Pastor Carlton Pearson. Many of us called him "Pastor Carlton."

Every song we sang during the opening praise and worship was a celebration, a positive declaration of faith. These songs reminded us both of the goodness of God and of who we were as Spirit-led Pentecostals, as Evangelicals on a mission. Our bodies were possessed with the energy of the words, most of which were simple and repetitive enough for anyone to sing, but clear and powerful enough to get the message across:

"Higher, Higher, Lift Jesus Higher!
Lower, Lower, Stump the Devil Lower!"

Once the atmosphere was fully drenched with the energy of our praise, Brenda Todd shifted to lead us in more meditative worship songs.

"To Him who sits on the throne, and unto the Lamb
Be all blessing, and glory, and honor, and power Foreeever!"

I settled into the divinity of that moment. My insides were warm and electrified with the fullness of God – knowing God, sensing God, feeling God. It was a stressful time in my life. I was a graduate student preparing to take several high-stakes exams, tests which placed my entire career in the balance. In the preceding months, I'd studied and prepared, fully aware that a certain element was entirely out of my control; my fate would be in the College Committee's hands. I'd prayed about it, asked God to let it go in my favor. Still, I was worried and anxious about the outcome. Would I have to find another job? Would we have to sell our house? Did we have enough in savings? Would we be able to pay our bills? In that holy moment, however, my hands raised, tears streaming down my face and staining the bodice of my fuchsia dress, I was overwhelmed by peaceful, blessed assurance.

In a seamless transition, Brenda Todd passed the microphone to Pastor Carlton, who continued to lead the song. Eyes were closed and heads were bowed when, at the last cadence of the song, he began to pray. As he closed his prayer with "Thy kingdom come, thy will be done," the choir director, Jesse Williams, brought us to our feet to sing the prayer response, whose words come from Psalm 121:

"Lord, I will lift
Mine eyes to the hills
Knowing my help
is coming from You"

As our choir sang "Total Praise," the words were relevant and alive, dynamic and meaningful to each one of us in a personal way. For me at that time, it was getting through school and finding stability in my career. For someone else, it was a marital struggle; for someone else, a sick child or a son or daughter in prison; for someone else, it was the grief of a tragic and unexpected loss. Our songs were our very own stories, our prayers and our testimonies told in harmonious collaboration.

We wore no choir robes, but often dressed in an array of jewel-toned colors – bright reds, bold purples, vivid greens, royal blues. Despite our immaculate grooming and apparel, something happened when we sang. We forgot about the congregation. We were not there to entertain the crowd, but to remind ourselves to enter into the presence of God. As I sang the line, "You are the source of my strength!" a lightning-strike of memory and a bolt of faith invaded my lungs. The truth of those words expanded my rib cage and came through my vocal chords; it was all of the affirmation I needed that everything in my life would turn out alright.

Jesse Williams, the choir director, was always immaculate in his grooming and dress. His hair was freshly barbered and his mustache and beard were meticulously shaven. He was usually color-coordinated from head-to-toe, wearing, for example, a purple suit and shoes in that exact shade of purple to match. He was barely over five feet and was not more than 130 pounds. Yet, each Sunday, he stood before the choir, a giant in his own right, pulling from us exactly the right phrasing and articulation, massaging each word of every song for maximum effect. As overcome as we were, we still had a job to do, and it was important to watch for his instruction, which was spontaneous and entirely in the moment. When we approached the closing "Amens" of the song, he mouthed to the soprano section, "Watch me!" At the final "Amen," he had us, the sopranos, to hold the ending tonic pitch for what seemed like an eternity while the other voices dropped out. When our breath was nearly exhausted, he brought the altos, tenors, and basses back in to resolve the closing chord to the grateful applause of an inspired congregation.

After the prayer response came the offertory. At this point in the service, we were reminded of the vast array of ministries and services that the church provided, and were encouraged to give generously, because "The seed that leaves your hand never leaves your life, but it goes into your future and multiplies." And gave, we did – to the tune of tens of thousands of dollars each week. We gave generously and joyfully, happy to support our cherished church home, its many ministries, and the salaries of dozens of well-paid Higher D staff.

There were many good reasons to attend Sunday morning service at Higher D. Of all its attractions, however, the main event at Higher D was Pastor Carlton's sermon. Part comedian, part scholar, part theologian, Pastor Carlton defied the gravity of expectation. He spoke sharply and quickly and loved to dissect Biblical terms for their original Hebrew and Greek meanings, taking us on an etymological journey that most of us found fascinating, whether or not we could actually keep up. He was also transparent about subjects that most ministers wouldn't touch. He addressed race from the pulpit in a way that put everyone at ease, telling many personal stories from his own experience, like this one:

> *When I was in college, one of my classmates commented, 'Hey Pearson, where did you get those lips?' I explained to him that when God formed the black man's lips, He took His time. All of His creative genius, all of His work went into forming lips that were plump, supple, well-crafted masterpieces. When it came to the white man's lips, God was tired, so he just took a razor blade and put a slit across his face.*

And the congregation erupted in laughter, even if they'd heard the story before. Pastor Carlton used this kind of humor in all his sermons while still sharing the message of the Gospel as we understood it. Although Higher D had no denominational affiliation, its creed was thoroughly Evangelical. The Church's mission – and our mission as church members – was to win souls to Christ. The end-goal of ministering to hurting people was to win them to Christ, to get them to believe as we did. For this reason, the culmination of every service at Higher D was the Altar Call, that moment when hurting and unsure people could publicly surrender their lives to God and become new creatures in Christ.

The Altar Call is a staple in most every Evangelical expression, and the script is usually the same. A product of the highly conservative Oral Roberts University and a protégé of Oral Roberts himself, Pastor Carlton followed the standard script. With music playing softly and our heads all bowed and our eyes closed, he asked us to examine our hearts. Anyone who felt sinful or unsure was invited to come forward. Those struggling with addiction, adultery, or homosexuality were invited to come forward. Anyone who otherwise doubted their salvation, who wanted to be sure of achieving Heaven and avoiding Hell, was invited to come forward. And those who simply needed spiritual reinforcement – extra strength for warding off the devil in the week to come – were invited to join the penitent, the hurting, and the backslidden at the altar. Waiting at the front of the church was a host of Altar Workers, trained counselors and ministers who prayed with each one seeking reassurance or salvation, and who offered assistance to anyone wishing to join the church.

With the Altar Call completed and those in need of extra ministry escorted to another room, the service concluded. But there was no mass exit from the building, no rush to be someplace else. Instead, we lingered, we visited, sometimes for an hour or more into the afternoon. This, after all, was family. Anyone of us was free to stay in the sanctuary as long as we wished, and there was no one to send us away; it was our home.

After the service, Pastor Carlton was typically accosted by throngs of people waiting to shake his hand, to ask for prayer, or to get a picture with him or his autograph on one of his many books or recordings. Many of us just stayed in the building to breathe in the residue of the previous hours' worth of celebration before continuing our conversations with friends out at Ryan's, Piccadilly, or one of the other restaurants in the vicinity of South Memorial Drive.

Sunday after Sunday, Higher D thus attracted sinners, inspired the faithful, electrified the city, and grew by leaps and bounds. I was from Gary, Indiana and came to Tulsa for college. After attending Higher D exclusively for years, I officially joined in 1994. James and I married there in 1996, and over the years, our lives had become so enmeshed with

Higher D that it was like an extension of the family room in our own home. My relatives, many of my coworkers, friends, and neighbors were also members of Higher D. As volunteers in the church's programs and ministries, we were there several times a week. In addition to Sunday service, I attended, at minimum, one or two mornings at 6am prayer, Tuesday evening choir practice, and Wednesday evening service. We lived five minutes away, so it was not unusual for us to find ourselves back at the church for other programs and events happening on other days of the week.

In many ways, Higher D was like its own small town, where everybody was somehow inextricably linked to everybody else. The reach of the church was so far and wide that it seemed to be the connective thread binding us in this complex, almost inescapable web. My sister was a beautician, and her shop was a defacto social hub for her clients, the overwhelming majority of whom were also members of Higher D. At the university where I taught, there were colleagues and students who were also members of Higher D. Several families in our subdivision were also members of Higher D. In addition to learning, in the run of things, that a neighbor, a colleague or a coworker also went to Higher D, there were the relationships we formed at Higher D itself – relationships that were fed and watered over time simply because so much of our lives were spent at church.

Sunday morning church service at Higher D, however, was like nothing else. It was a perfect storm where tears and laughter, comedy and Christianity, faith, family, and Holy Ghost fire all came together. For our mix of backgrounds and ethnicities, it was a sort of Utopia. Within those walls, we not only worshiped together, but also loved and married across racial lines. We held each other's children, shared meals at each other's homes, surrounded one another in times of sorrow, and met up together again on Sunday morning, when we were all lifted once more.

---

1. David Smith, Brenda Todd, and Jesse Williams were highly visible ministers at Higher Dimensions for many years, and they are referenced throughout by name. Other names, however, have been changed.

CHAPTER 3

"It was in the back, right next to a pole..."

-Cassandra

I stumbled into Higher D in 1995-wounded, broken, destitute, barely alive. I had never heard of Carlton Pearson before. I didn't know he was a Christian celebrity, and I didn't know of his connection to Oral Roberts. I had never seen him on television, I didn't know he was a black man, and I had no affiliation with anyone in his circle. Although I was a native Tulsan, and Carlton Pearson had been in Tulsa for about twenty years at that time, I had no awareness whatsoever of him or his church. I ended up at Higher D because I was just trying to survive.

I was thirty-four years old at the time and going through the most broken I'd ever been in my life. It was during this period that I was just beginning to understand the gnawing, agonizing pain that was constantly with me. I come from a large family and am the twelfth of fourteen children. I was fortunate to grow up in a family with parents who were determined to teach us about the good things in life despite all the challenges they themselves faced. There was something about my childhood that always seemed calm and peaceful. No problem seemed beyond fixing. Momma had a way of making all of us feel special, but she was no joke. In fact, I think she invented tough love! We lived in a rural area of Oklahoma about twenty-five miles outside of town. For us, social life was limited to home, school, and church. Momma ran an orderly, disciplined house. Everyone danced to the beat of her drum and we children always understood our boundaries. She loved us all, but treated each one of us as individuals. Regardless of how big the problem, she always seemed to have the answer, but was always intent on teaching us to think for ourselves. She stood for what she believed in even when she had to stand alone. To me, she represented wholeness.

My father was my hero. Standing about six feet, four inches, he was a soft-spoken man of his word, and he expected others to keep theirs. A quiet man who was not easily impressed by anything, he was firm in his convictions, yet loving and caring. Outsiders had but one time to cross him, and if they did, they would never get that chance again. He believed in minding his business and that everyone else should mind theirs. He didn't care for hypocrites and never concerned himself with the opinions of others. To me, my father represented authority.

I graduated from high school, moved out of my parents'

house, and was married by the age of eighteen. My husband was six years my senior and from a background different than mine, but he still fit right in with my family as if he had always been a part of us. We were a close-knit family and remained close even as adults. Our Sunday tradition was gathering at my parents' house for dinner. The entire family came, and afterwards we sat around and talked and laughed for hours. Sunday dinner at Momma's was as certain as the sun rising in the sky. I thought life would be this way forever.

It was New Year's Day, 1982. My family received some news that changed our lives forever. Our father, my hero, my Rock of Gibraltar, was found dead. Without warning, without a hint, without a clue of any problem in his body, at the age of sixty-two years old, he was gone. Just like that. This giant of a man, who was the sole provider and protector of my family, fell to his death and left us forever. It was the first day of the new year and the first day of the year that he would retire from thirty-two years of work; it was the first day of the year that his fourteenth child would graduate from high school, and the first day of the worst memory of my life.

My New Year's Day began with me waking up to cook breakfast. Shortly afterward, I left my home to pick up my daughter from my sister's house. When I arrived there, my niece met me at the front door. She told me they received a call that my father had a heart attack. Those words stopped me in my tracks. I immediately felt my heart racing; suddenly, I couldn't get enough air to breathe. Trying to remain calm and assuming he'd been taken to a hospital, I asked which hospital he'd been taken to, but she didn't know. So I called my parents' house and a lady from the church answered. I asked about the hospital to which he'd been transported.

She asked me who I was, and when I replied, then she said, "Honey they are not taking him to a hospital. They are taking him straight to Jack's." Then she paused and said, "You need to be on your way out here." As I hung up the phone in what seemed like slow motion, I tried to digest what she said. It was as if I had stepped outside myself and entered the twilight zone.

Jack's was a local funeral home and I was trying to figure out if what I heard was really what she said. I remember feeling outside of myself, almost as if in a dream. I remember thinking maybe the lady on the other end of the phone meant to say they were taking my dad to Hillcrest, or to St. John's or to St. Francis, one of the nearby hospitals. Maybe I just heard it wrong. The conversation kept playing over and over in my head.

The forty-minute ride to my parents' house seemed like eternity. I needed to get there fast. I needed to know that my father was alright; I needed to see that my mother was alright. Oh, how I prayed that everything would be okay. The closer we got to the house, the faster my heart pounded. As we approached the curve just before the house, I could see several cars parked in the yard. I saw the ambulance backed up to the front door. I wondered why it was still sitting there.

When we finally pulled into the main driveway, I could see the white coroner's car backed up to the back door of the house. It was at that very moment I realized that my worst fear had come true.

As I walked through the front door of my parents' home, with tears flooding my eyes I saw only images of people sitting and standing around in the living room. I remember seeing and embracing the minister from my church without ever saying a word. I remember my sister giving me a wet rag to wipe my face, then I walked toward the kitchen to find my mother. I needed to see her face to know what to do. When I found her, she was coming from the bathroom where my father's body was still laying on the floor. The medical examiner had just pronounced him dead. They were preparing to take his body out. I will never forget the pain I saw in my mother's big brown eyes as she made her way toward me. We embraced, and I broke into tears, and I heard her say in a faint voice, "He's gone now. . . he's gone now." We stood together and watched as they began to lift him from the floor. My father was large in stature and it took six men to remove his body from the house. They took him out through the back door and loaded his lifeless body into the hearse. I couldn't believe my hero was gone. I couldn't believe this was happening. I prayed it was just a bad dream and wanted desperately to wake up. I was twenty-one years old and felt my foundation had been ripped from beneath me. What would we do without my father? How could we live without ever seeing him again? Who would protect us now? Why did he have to die? How could we ever be okay again?

The time between my father's death and the day of the funeral was a blur. Night after night, I sat up gazing out the window wondering how we would recover. The funeral service took place on what seemed to be the coldest day in history. The church was packed with people in the sanctuary, and the overflow filled the dining area. There was standing room only, and some waited outside in the cold. Remarkably, while comforting us, my mother handled all the arrangements with grace.

Many dark days followed, and things were never the same. We watched our mother quietly go through a painful adjustment period. After forty-two years of marriage, she was starting the slow, agonizing process of learning to live without my father. We did our best to take care of her, and she knew that. She always showed appreciation for all that we did.

Things seemed to get a little easier when I realized that we still had our mom and that she was going to be okay. She had always been careful not to show signs of hopelessness and did all she could to restore a sense of normalcy. She was the glue that held us together all our lives. She continued to be the glue that would keep us together in this season.

Momma eventually returned to her busy schedule tending to our family, her community work, and the affairs at church. Sunday dinners at Momma's house resumed in full force.

Although she tried to keep busy, I can recall many times that I saw her gazing out into space with a certain expression on her face. This let me know that whatever she was thinking about was far beyond my reach. Nevertheless, I could feel what she didn't have to say.

It was in 1985 after a Sunday dinner when my sisters and I gathered in my mom's bedroom to talk with her like we often did. The house was noisy as usual with kids and conversations. On this particular Sunday, we were due back in church for an evening service, so Momma went to her room to change clothes and freshen up her makeup. When she sat down on her bench in front of her dresser her face was glistening with perspiration. I remember my sister Sheila gently patting the perspiration from her forehead with a rag just before my mom began to powder her face. I was standing behind my mom styling her hair as she looked on in the mirror in front of her. Then I heard Sheila ask, "What is this?"

I then turned to look at what she was talking about. I noticed a dark patch on my mom's chest slightly above her breast and what looked like a swelling or something protruding just beneath the skin. She didn't say much about it. She simply brushed her hand over it and said, "I'm going to see about this thing tomorrow" and left it at that. She continued getting dressed. We went to church. Together with Momma and my sisters, we were the church choir, so we went to the service that night and sang as we normally did. Nothing else was said about it on that day.

Within weeks, my mom started regular treatments for breast cancer. She eventually had surgery. My sisters and I rotated caring for our mom, and it was strange for us to see her looking so fragile. After the surgery, however, things began to look up. She entered remission, regained her strength, adjusted to her new normal, and resumed living life. Momma traveled quite a bit during this period. She had no problem hopping on a plane and flying the friendly skies. She loved traveling and we were glad to see her branching out and enjoying a little adventure. For nearly three years following her surgery, Momma had no problems. She was active, happy, and living life to the fullest.

But the cancer returned. I specifically remember sensing it had returned before she ever mentioned it to us. It was Thanksgiving Day, 1987, and the house was filled with family and holiday cheer. I happened to look across the room and caught a glimpse of Momma's face and in her eyes was something I'd never seen before. She was scanning the room as if she was taking it all in. By the look in her eyes, I knew that she was thinking it would be the last Thanksgiving she would live to see. It was a disturbing moment for me, so I called out to her and started a conversation to distract her from her thoughts. This second bout was much more intense. The cancer was more aggressive and Momma's treatments were more frequent. My sisters and I organized our lives around her doctors' appointments, never missing a beat.

Momma's sister passed away in January 1988, and on

the evening that we told her about it, she immediately went into planning mode. Remarkably, she planned and coordinated her sister's funeral service right from her own sick bed; she even gathered the strength to attend the service. On that very same day, after returning home from my aunt's funeral, my mom said, "Now bring my book with my insurance papers in it and let's get started planning mine."

Sunday morning, February 28, 1988, I woke up in the chair where I had fallen asleep the night before. This chair was in the corner of the bedroom where my mother slept in my sister's house. She was even weaker by now, so we never left her alone for any length of time. It was my turn to keep watch over her during the night, so I sent my husband and kids home for the evening and made myself comfortable in the room with her. The TV was on throughout the night and I watched her dose off and on. She woke up about every hour to look over at me as though she was checking to make sure I was still in the room.

It wasn't long before everybody in the house was up and moving about, and as the morning passed, my siblings and their families started to arrive. I went home to shower and change, planning to take a brief nap before heading back over to spend the rest of the afternoon with my family. I was barely home, when, for some unknown reason, I was startled out of my sleep. I jumped up, got dressed, put my shoes on and told my husband that I needed to go back to my sister's house. With a perplexed look on his face, he said to me, "But you just left there," and I said, "I know, but I need to get back right now." Soon we were on our way.

When we arrived, everybody was still there. I walked into the room and two of my sisters and sister-in-law were visiting with my mom. I was asked to come and help maneuver my mom around so that she could get cleaned up for the day. I remember my mom reaching out with her arms stretched motioning for one of us to help her to sit up. I walked over next to her bed and took her hands and gently began pulling her forward toward me. Suddenly, she groaned as if that motion was painful for her. I immediately stopped and asked her if that was hurting her, and she said yes. So we laid her back down, and I leaned over the bed across her body, placing both my arms around her back (in a bear hug) and began gently lifting her forward. As I did, one of my sisters cried out from behind me, "Momma, Momma's eyes!" And with my arms still wrapped around her, I felt her going limp in my embrace.

My mother died that day, right there in that room with us, in my arms, in a house filled with people who loved her. There was an energy shift in those moments. I didn't know if I was sleep or awake. When the paramedics arrived, I left the room to comfort the rest of the family. The house was filled with tears and no one knew exactly what to do. The paramedics spent about twenty minutes in the room before taking my mother out. When they were almost out the door with her, my son, who was nine years old at the time, yelled out through his tears, "Wait a minute, wait a minute! I gotta say something!" When they stopped, he said: "Grandma, I'm gonna miss you." The cries of our grief-stricken family could be heard throughout the house.

My father died in 1982. Before I could fully come to grips with his death, my mother died just six years later in 1988. It's heart-wrenching when someone you really love dies. Seems the more you love them, the harder your loss, and the harder your loss, the longer your grieving period; somehow that doesn't seem fair. Accepting the fact that you will never see, hear, or touch that person again is a reality that none of us wants to face. Until it's your turn to go through a loss of this magnitude, you can never truly understand the depth of sorrow that you are capable of feeling. When my parents left this planet, the world became a different place for me. I realized that who I was would never mean as much to anyone else living. My parents' love for me was the only sure thing in my life; so the pain that I felt was magnified. It was draining and debilitating, the first thing I felt when I opened my eyes in the morning and the last thing I felt before falling asleep at night.

In the years following my mother's death, I held on with no progression forward. And I could feel myself slipping into someone I didn't know. I was walking through the most tender, oddest, uncomfortable, unwelcomed, unsure, lost period in my life. My one goal was to keep breathing until something happened, until something changed. It didn't even matter what, as long as it would take the pain away. The pain compelled me to walk away from everything I once knew, including the church where I'd been a member since birth and a seventeen-year marriage. In my weakened state, I was desperate and determined to find peace by any means necessary.

On a Sunday morning, sometime in 1995, I stumbled upon Higher Dimensions Church. It was the fourth church, in four Sundays, that I had visited in Tulsa after taking a three-year hiatus from my own church, for the first time in my life. When I entered the Higher Dimensions building, I was amazed at its size and its design. I remember thinking that I'd never fit in at a church with that many people. On that Sunday, there was a guest speaker who gave the message because Carlton Pearson was out of town. I don't remember the name of the guest speaker, or the title of his sermon, but I do remember that it touched on many of the things that I was experiencing.

What I remember most about my first visit was the usher that greeted me. I remember the way she treated me in those first few moments after I arrived through the doors. I distinctly remember her vibration, her gentleness, and her hug. Having never laid eyes on me before and knowing nothing of my story, she made me feel as though she understood everything I was going through. Her loving presence reassured me that I had come to the right place. She was kind, patient, attentive, and had a transparent and welcoming spirit that I will never forget. She did all she could to find just the right seat for me. I didn't want to sit near the front or the middle or near anybody, really; instead, I wanted to sit somewhere in the back so that I could observe from a distance. Without judgement, hesitation, or reservation, she found the perfect seat and made sure I was comfortable sitting there. I will never forget thinking how perfect that seat really was. It was in the back, right next to a pole, away from everybody else, but close enough to the door, so that if I chose to leave I could do so without being a distraction. As it turned out, however, I didn't leave. I decided to stay for the duration of the service.

Along with the hospitality and the message, the music embraced me and was like salve to my soul. When the choir stood to sing, I was completely removed from my dark reality into a place of tranquility, and I knew right then I had reached the place I was looking for.

From that Sunday on, I was a regular attendee at Higher Dimensions Church. At my home church, I had always been front- and-center; at Higher D, however, I continued sitting in the back near the door for quite some time. I just watched and listened and grabbed every bit of healing I could rub on my broken heart and wounded spirit. I may have seen that usher three or four more times in passing during services. But I never got to know anything else about her before noticing she wasn't there any longer. Maybe she was an angel. Who knows.

Carlton Pearson traveled quite a bit back in those days, so it must have been my third visit to the church when I actually got to hear him speak for the first time. But oh! – when I did hear him speak, it was like nothing I'd ever heard before. It was almost like God had stepped out of Heaven to talk directly to me about the pain in my heart. Never had I heard a message so on point, so tailored for me. The sermon was much like the precision of a heart surgeon's hand removing blockages. I felt like Carlton Pearson was speaking directly to me about me, although I was a complete stranger to him. This went on Sunday after Sunday. His messages described right where I was. He brought scripture to life and added countless personal stories. I came to understand how all of my experiences really did work together for my good. I felt myself healing from the very first message I heard and began evolving with every sermon thereafter. I felt a sense of peace every time I walked through those doors. Although I continued to sit in my favorite spot near the back of the church, I was having a powerful breakthrough!

Carlton Pearson was an extraordinary orator, and everyone loved his storytelling as much as they loved his intelligence and command of the Scriptures. He was also a comedian, often imitating Redd Foxx from the television sitcom *Sanford and Son*. He loved sharing this favorite quote from his eighty-year-old grandfather: "General rule, man's a fool. When it's hot, he wants it cool. When it's cool, he wants it hot. He always wants what he haven't got!" He had a unique way of using humor to drive home powerful truths.

Each Sunday before I left, I would stop in the church book store to purchase a tape of the message to take home and play as many times as needed. It was like medication for my soul. There were times when I would lay on the floor, in front of my stereo, and listen to the message over and over again throughout the week. It was the only thing that I'd found in all my grieving years that finally worked for me.

It was November 26, 1995 when Carlton Pearson preached a message titled *The God Who Is Able*. I remember the specifics of this sermon because it was the message that persuaded me to trust God with *all* of me. He expounded on the scripture about how God could do "exceedingly and abundantly above all that I could ask or think according to the power that was at work within me" (Ephesians 3:20, KJV). He emphasized that God was able to keep me and settle me through whatever situation I had suffered. God could exceed anything I could think to ask Him, all because of *the power that was already inside of me*. That was my "AHA!" moment! It opened my mind up to the vastness of God's love for me. I came to understand that God had equipped me for my dark days and disappointments, my hurt and my grief. Those words, that moment, that atmosphere caused me to release my doubt and to see God from a different angle. I started to understand that he'd already created me with the ability and power to change my situation by changing my thinking about the situation. That very moment "de-victimized" me.

I purchased the tape after the service, and I played it repeatedly for weeks, crying every time I heard it, realizing that I was meant to be exactly where I was to receive it exactly as I did. Today I still have that original tape. After hundreds of hearings, it is too worn for me to play; yet, I keep it as a monument and testament of my journey to wholeness.

Higher D was alive and popping back then. Special guest speakers, Gospel celebrity singers, and other high-profile people came frequently. My entire preoccupation, however, was on my own emotional healing. I didn't really focus on anything outside of that. I was so grateful to feel my pain subsiding as time passed. The atmosphere on Sundays refueled me so much that I began sitting in on Tuesday night choir rehearsals just to listen in and be present.

Every choir rehearsal began with a praise and worship hour during which the members of the choir engaged in close communion with God. They poured out their hearts to God in prayer, seeking God's presence for the coming week. They sang song after song and prayed and cried and seemed to bring every one of their personal issues into the room. I saw it as a cleansing hour for everyone there. The choir had sixty or more voices at that time, a far cry from what I was used to at my home church. The Higher D musicians were the best I'd ever heard in the land. I had been a spectator at Tuesday night choir rehearsals for several weeks when, one evening, someone asked if I'd like to sing with the mass choir for the upcoming, week-long Azusa Conference that was to be held at the Oral Roberts Mabee Center in Tulsa. Of course, I excitedly answered "Yes!", even though I had no idea what that meant or what it would require of me.

Although I was excited about the prospect of singing for Azusa, my focus really remained on my healing. Up until this point, I was happy to be inconspicuous. I was satisfied with just sitting back and taking it all in. I never missed a Sunday service at Higher Dimensions during this period. I never missed buying my weekly tape of the sermon. I bought an assortment of audio tapes and books by the many guest speakers who would frequent our church. I rushed home from work every evening, closed myself in to read a book or to listen to a sermon. I was determined to find my way back again.

CHAPTER 4

"… that glorious week in April of Heaven on Earth."

— Teresa

I was a college student when I first attended Higher D in 1988. Originally from Indiana, I relocated to Oklahoma to attend graduate school at the University of Tulsa. I was living with my sister and brother-in-law at the time. Since Higher D was their church, it was natural for me to follow them there and to adopt the church as my own. After finishing my master's degree, I moved away for a few years, but returned to Tulsa in 1994, which was the year I officially joined Higher D in my own right.

Like Pastor Carlton, my religious background was in the Church of God in Christ (COGIC), the largest black Pentecostal denomination in the world. While growing up, I attended services several times each week with my family. The address of Open Door Church of God in Christ is still indelibly etched in my memory: 2134 West Fifth Avenue in Gary, Indiana. We were called "sanctified," as we were easily identifiable by our strict behavioral standards and modest dress. As members of the "sanctified" church, we embraced a very literal interpretation of the Bible. For example, we took seriously the Old-Testament rule forbidding women to wear "anything that pertaineth to a man." Therefore, my sisters and I wore dresses every day of our young lives, rain or shine, in sweltering heat and in freezing temperatures. We wore dresses to the beach and to the park, sincerely believing that we were doing God's will. We didn't go to parties, to movies, or to dances; we didn't wear makeup or jewelry; we didn't drink, smoke, cuss, or fornicate. We proudly kept ourselves separate from "sinners," never socializing with them, and engaging with them only for business or to convert them.

We were raised on a regular diet of hellfire-and-brimstone preaching, and spent almost as many hours in church as we spent in school. There was Sunday School at 10:00, Sunday service at noon, and Sunday evening service at 7:30. There was Tuesday evening service, choir practice on Thursday evening, Friday evening service, and Saturday evening Youth service. Each of these weekly encounters lasted about two hours or more. As severe and restricted as our lives may have been, my sisters and I loved going to church. It felt incredibly safe there. Going to church was like visiting family. It was the center of our social lives, and it embodied all that we were free to do without fear of hell. Church was where we were reaffirmed, time and again, in the "rightness" of our beliefs; where, within our small and strange circle, we could be our own definition of *normal*.

Himself born and raised in the sanctified church, Pastor Carlton knew well the intense piety of that particular religion. Along with the rules and regulations, however, the sanctified church was the source of a distinctive, fiery style of music and praise. Pastor Carlton was very proud of his COGIC roots and Pentecostal background, which were on full display at Higher D—the music, the worship, the interpretation of scripture. And, of course, this was all familiar to me. I was still in grad school—this time, pursuing a Ph.D.—when I moved to Tulsa and officially joined Higher D in 1994. With its smorgasbord of programs, excellent music, progressive and multiracial congregation, and charismatic and popular pastor, there was nothing not to love about this church. Like the multitudes of black college types who flocked there each week, I loved that the church seemed to blend a certain intellectual orientation with the spiritual fire. I felt at home there.

Despite the many blessings it offered, Higher D also had a reputation for being, well, "uppity." In the city of Tulsa, there is a definite geographical divide separating blacks who live on the North Side and those who live south of Admiral Boulevard. Blacks who lived North were usually native Tulsans whose forefathers had bitter memories of the infamous 1921 Race Massacre. Blacks who lived on the South Side of town , by contrast, were often transplants from other cities who came to attend one of the universities or Bible colleges in the area. One particular evening, I was made strikingly aware of this divide, as North Tulsa blacks often had a certain suspicion of us relative newcomers to the city who lived and worshipped on the South side.

I was at a holiday gathering in North Tulsa at the invitation of a college friend of mine. Most of the people there were unfamiliar to me, so we engaged in small talk and pleasant conversation. Then, the topic shifted to, "So, where do you live?" and "Where do you worship?" Naively, I answered that I lived in South Tulsa, and that I attended Higher D. Suddenly, I felt like a convicted criminal under a spotlight. A woman at the party (let's call her Pat), didn't hold back. Immediately, she condemned me, labeling me a traitor for abandoning North Tulsa's black community. She ridiculed me for attending Higher D, that church full of arrogant and "stuck-up" members with a crowd too big to do any good. Pat knew nothing about me except my name and my church. This, in her eyes, was all the information she needed to size me up as the enemy.

I later came to realize that the religious establishment of North Tulsa viewed Higher D as unfair competition. The charismatic young pastor and multicultural congregation were attracting many North Tulsa black residents—and their weekly offerings—away from the more traditional churches that had always relied upon them for support and survival. But not everyone shared Pat's negative and inaccurate view of Higher Dimensions. Pastor Carlton was deeply invested in bringing people together, despite their differences. The annual Azusa Conference was a major gathering, uniting not only Christians from around the city but from around the world.

Pastor Carlton was a visionary. Restless and forward-thinking, his presence extended well beyond the confines of 8621 South Memorial Drive. By the early 1990s, Pastor Carlton's appearances on Christian television, and his popularity through his books, and cassette and VHS tapes gave him the kind of exposure that would have been the envy of any young pastor his age. And this was all before the dawn of the Digital Age. From its inception in the Jenks storefront, Higher D had always been an anomaly, this multiracial, multiethnic gathering, unique in its embrace of African-American leadership. As an intelligent, non-threatening black man who was funny as hell, Pastor Carlton was a godsend for the Evangelical brand.

Yet, his Evangelical background was decidedly different than what most white people knew or understood. Pastor Carlton's COGIC background was thoroughly and distinctively African-American in its heritage, flavor, and sensibility. A large segment of his following—myself included—shared those roots. The COGIC expression was birthed out of the turn-of-the-twentieth-century Azusa Street Revival and developed rapidly during the very difficult years of racial segregation. From its slave heritage, COGIC congregations preserved the practice of literally calling down the very presence of God, of actually seeking to feel God in an experiential and obvious way. This was about more than getting to Heaven someday in the hereafter; this, instead, was Holy Empowerment to make life work right here, right now on this earth.

Along with the God experience, COGIC people emphasized clean, "sanctified" living. In its most extreme form, this included prohibitions (for women) against the wearing of slacks or putting on makeup. Although the rules about slacks and makeup had become quite relaxed, the sensing of God's presence was still indispensable.

More than any African-American preacher before him, Pastor Carlton created a space for black Pentecostals at the table where the Evangelical elite held court. Most other black ministers were focused on preserving their time-honored traditions. Pastor Carlton, by contrast, sought a new frontier. He presented his Pentecostal blackness as a missing ingredient that attracted the notice of white Evangelical star power: Kenneth Hagin, Kenneth Copeland, Marilyn Hickey, Joyce Meyer, Oral Roberts, TL Osborn, and others. These all knew Pastor Carlton and respected his influence. And when Pastor Carlton had the idea to present his unique style of worship in a major annual conference, some of these heavy-hitters would grace its stage.

Azusa was a massive gathering of some forty thousand participants from around the world. This mega-revival was held each year over a six-day period in April. It was not just a conference, however; at Higher D, Azusa was an entire season. It was the Higher D church membership that came together to make the conference happen. For the most part, our church members served as the conference's coordinators, publicists, ushers, greeters, drivers, technicians, hosts, musicians, childcare workers, and setup and tear-down crew for the entire event. It was also Higher D that helped to front the major expenses of the conference in anticipation of the thousands who traveled to Tulsa every year to attend. Our offerings provided the down payments on blocks of hotel rooms and other necessities that needed to be secured in advance. The conference was held at the Mabee Center on the campus of Oral Roberts University.

Although Pastor Carlton founded and convened the Azusa conference, he most often served as its host and facilitator rather than as the main speaker himself. Although he was the founder and the glue that held the conference together, Azusa really became a showcase for both well-known and little-known Christian talent. It was at the Azusa Conference in 1992, for example, that a then unknown T.D. Jakes first received the exposure that he would later thank for his superstardom. Azusa, therefore, was both Sunday morning at Higher D on steroids, and the most important connection you could get if you wanted to advance your ministry.

Azusa season always started in late February and culminated with the end of the conference the week after Easter in April. For me, the excitement began with the mass choir rehearsals that invited participation from singers from around the city and state. Unlike the Higher D choir, which was audition-only, the Azusa Mass Choir was open invitation to anyone willing to learn the words to the songs and attend the rehearsals on Tuesday and Thursday evenings. Each year, friends from Rhema Bible Church, Friendship Baptist, the Love Center, North Side Church of God in Christ, and many other area churches united with us to form the Azusa Mass Choir.

Usually numbering between two hundred and three hundred singers, the Azusa Mass Choir's rehearsal space was set up in our fellowship hall, which we called the Destiny Center. We started rehearsals at 7pm sharp with praise and worship led by minister of music Alvin Fruga (pronounced Froo Jay.) While we sang praise songs, people filed in to find their seats, some still wearing their work clothes, others smelling like the dinner they'd just cooked before leaving home. We were always excited to reunite with old friends from other churches returning as they'd done every year. We were also thrilled to welcome new friends joining with us to sing for the first time. Section leaders divided sopranos, altos, tenors, and basses into their appropriate places and distributed folders containing song lyrics and important information about the conference. Experienced choir members showed the newcomers the ropes, with blacks helping whites to sway on beat and clap on two and four instead of on one and three. Rehearsal was full of starts and stops, to work on enunciating every word, to get the intonation, the harmony, and the syncopation right.

And then, as always, there was free reign for the Spirit to fall on us and transport us into a place of reverent worship. Over the years, we prepared hundreds of songs, but a few stood out. There is a chorus we sang that declared, "Jehovah Jireh, He's the God who provides for us." When your life experience bears out that truth—as was the case with me—it is impossible to sing that line and not become overwhelmed. It is impossible to avoid reflecting upon your own personal evidence of God as Provider. The song lyrics are no longer static imprints on a page; the very letters that make up the words become alive and float into the atmosphere and they transform the space into something indescribably rapturous and beautiful. When hundreds of singers are thus gathered in such reflection, each one drawn into his or her own worshipful thanksgiving, there is an oblivion to time and space that just takes over. So it was at many of our Higher D choir rehearsals, and so it was when the mass choir rehearsed in preparation for Azusa.

Pastor Alvin was assisted by an entire battalion of musicians. Some of our songs were old, traditional, and familiar. Many others, however, were hot-off-the-press originals, composed by Alvin Fruga, David Smith, or Jesse Williams. When we sang, our many voices blended into one majestic sound, our hearts turned Heavenward in worship, our thoughts envisioning that glorious week in April of

Heaven on Earth.

Like Sunday morning service at Higher D, the intensity and excitement of Azusa week was palpable, almost overwhelming. As did many others, I scheduled to be off work that week, wishing for nothing to interfere with my ability to soak up every drop of that divine experience. The conference included workshops and various events throughout the day, but the main events were the evening services. The doors to the Mabee Center opened at 6pm, with opening prayer starting at 6:30. By 4:30pm, however, the line outside of the building was already beginning to form. Seating was open, affording the best spots to those who arrived early. I joined the line by 4:45, carrying stacks of books and Bibles under my arm so that I could use them to save good seats for my own family and out-of-town guests. This was a common practice at every Azusa, an easy way to indicate what seats were taken and which were still available.

The line behind me grew to be much longer than the line ahead of me. They had come from every region of the country and from many parts of the world--blacks and whites, Latinos and Native Americans, East Indian men and women in their tunics and saris, Africans from Ghana, Nigeria, Senegal, and the Ivory Coast, all in the explosive colors and patterns of their native dress. We stood in the line, singing, praising, anticipating, until the doors were finally opened at 6:00pm.

The interior of the Mabee Center auditorium was like a giant, slightly oblong bowl, a stadium formation that held about ten thousand, with about a thousand of those seats on the main floor. An elevated platform skirted in black was constructed to form the stage where the musicians and pulpit guests sat, and behind them were about ten rows of the stadium seats designated for the mass choir. In gigantic, iridescent letters, the word AZUSA was suspended from the ceiling above the stage.

Once the doors opened, I joined the mad rush to stake my claim of the best seats I could find for my family. I quickly pointed them to their reserved places before rushing off to the restroom for one last stop before taking my place in the choir stand. The evening services were video-recorded, so choir members understood the necessity of being in place for the entire service. Once seated there, it could be midnight before I'd get to the restroom again. This was no more of an issue for me, however, than the hours-long discomfort of tight pantyhose and high-heeled shoes. I didn't want to miss anything, so it never crossed my mind to move from my assigned place.

The speakers at Azusa were the royalty of Pentecost and gospel music. Everybody who was anybody might be there, from artists like Fred Hammond, Andre Crouch, Donnie McClurkin, Shirley Caesar, Beverly Crawford, Richard Smallwood, Yolanda Adams, Kirk Franklin, to preachers ranging from TD Jakes, to Juanita Bynum, to Joyce Meyer, to Kenneth Copland. Pastor Carlton always introduced newcomers alongside these Christian celebrities, graciously giving them the kind of exposure they couldn't possibly get elsewhere.

For several years, the music of the Azusa conferences was recorded and released as *Live at Azusa* CDs and videos. After the conference was over and the Azusa mass choir disbursed, the members of the Higher D choir left their day jobs to gather at a local recording studio to overdub the live music. The studio, nicknamed "The Church Studio," had actually been that in its former life. It was on Third & Trenton toward the North Side of Tulsa, and its flight of stone steps led to a pair of wooden double doors that were once the entrance to its sanctuary.

Inside of the former-sanctuary were microphones on stands and suspended from the ceiling, a multi-colored assortment of headphones, and various instruments – both dead and functional – scattered about. The floors had the fade marks and imprints of where pews had once been. The walls were decorated with the posters of moderately-famous regional talent that had recorded there. At the back of the room was the large glass booth with all of the recording gizmos and technological bells and whistles. All that remained of the building's former life as a church was the distinctive smell of moldy, varnished wood so typical of old buildings. This was an entirely functional space, one devoted solely to the business of making music.

The Azusa recordings were hard work. We welcomed the opportunity, however, to relive those songs and to prepare them for the world to hear. We'd each rush away from our various places of employment to meet at the studio at 6pm to check microphones and levels. Pastor David stood behind the sound-proof glass booth, signaling directions. As soon as the sound of the master recording came through our headphones, we were transported back to that glorious week at the Mabee Center. Right there in the studio, our souls tapped into the fire of the conference and suddenly, the Holy Ghost was there again. As we sang, layering our voices over the recording, we gained the strength and the anointing for the multiple takes that a single portion of a track might require to get it right. In between takes, there was prayer and praise, much laughter, conversation, and joke-cracking, losing focus and then quickly refocusing, determined to get the job done. We'd work until 10 or so, break to share a meal of Kentucky Fried Chicken, work another couple of hours, and then get home as late as 1:30 or 2:00 in the morning. We'd go back to the studio the next night and do the same thing all over again until every track was finished and the project was completed. *Live at Azusa* Nos. 1, 2, 3, and 4 are still popular and you can buy them on Amazon. And then there was *Azusa Praise: We Cry Out,* recorded in 2002. That is another story.

CHAPTER 5

"I'd come a long way from my safe and inconspicuous place..."

– Cassandra

I came from a small country church; so the non-denominational, "mega-church" experience took some getting used to. Everything about it was different, from the Sunday service format, to the assigned "armor-bearers," and even to the way Bishop Pearson and his wife, Gina, were approached. This all seemed a bit much in the beginning. And like most churches of its enormous size, Higher Dimensions had cliques, favorites, and "elite" groups that were obvious to anyone observing. In general, I suppose people meant well; but arrogance and superficiality showed up some of that time. I knew that I had to walk softly coming in; so I quietly observed those in charge, those who thought they were in charge, and the way things were done. I tried to understand the reasoning behind all of the formalities and the red tape. The things I didn't understand immediately, I put on the back burner. I was determined not to allow anything to distract me from my new lease on life or to interrupt my healing flow.

Bishop Pearson and Gina had only been married three years when I arrived at Higher Dimensions. As far as I could tell, it seemed they had been married forever. I had no reason to assume otherwise, since all of the ministers I knew from my own background were married men. I came to learn, however, that he was over forty and basically a newlywed. Before long, I began hearing stories about how some of the single women in the church constantly and boldly pursued him when he was available. I was grateful that fiasco was over.

Even though he was faithfully married to Gina, however, not everyone's interpretation of Bishop Pearson's vibes were healthy ones. I soon learned about the misguided, unfortunate women still in our congregation who seemed to read far more into his genuine kindness than was ever there. We had our usual "crazies" at Higher Dimensions, as I called them. They were present on a regular basis and would stop at nothing to get Bishop Pearson's attention despite the many warnings from staff and security. To think this type of behavior existed in church was beyond foreign to me. It would have been most fitting in a nightclub, perhaps after a few drinks. Nevertheless, boundaries were clearly set and boundaries were sometimes clearly ignored. As time went on, I came to realize that the antics of desperate women were quite common in megachurches. It wasn't just happening to the Senior ministers; it was just more obvious and occurred more often with the pastor and with the more visible leaders in the church.

I knew very little about Bishop Pearson and Gina personally back then. My only experience with either of them was during the week at the church. I just knew that Gina was one of the most beautiful women I'd ever seen. They were adorable together. They called her the "First Lady," a title that I was unaccustomed to using. Back in the little church where I came from, our pastor's wife was called "the pastor's wife." With all due respect for her position, the pastor's wife was on a level playing field with all of the rest of us. She did everything that we did. When I swept the floor, she held the dust pan. No one addressed her as "Your-Highness" and she received no special treatment. It was just how things were. I came to understand, however, that at a megachurch like Higher D, the pastor's wife was put on a pedestal.

Bishop Pearson talked about Gina and their relationship often in his sermons. It always made me feel good to think they were happy together. Whenever I heard him talk about how much he loved her and their son, Julian, it was comforting and reassuring to me in the same way that I felt comforted by the love of my own family. And when their daughter Majeste' came along, it seemed like the love was intensified. Over time, observing the dynamics between Bishop Pearson, Gina, and members of the staff answered many questions that I held inside but never asked out loud. Things are never quite what they seem. Higher Dimensions church, like all church families, had its share of trouble-spots. The staff knew that things weren't perfect, but I respected them for never talking publicly about those flaws.

My decision to sing with the Azusa Mass Choir in 1996 opened a whole new world for me. I wasn't a part of the Higher Dimensions core choir just yet. Joining the Azusa Mass Choir, however, gave me an opportunity to sing along with the Higher D choir, as well as with other singers from the local community. This experience was one that I will always treasure because, along with Bishop Pearson's preaching, it gave me a sense of healing and restoration from the intense grief of losing my parents. I'd come a long way from my safe and inconspicuous place in the back of the sanctuary, beside the pole, near the exit.

Every night of the Azusa Conference was like a double scoop of whatever I needed God to be, whatever I needed the world to be, and whatever I needed me to be. It is amazing what the presence of God can do when you're open to it from every direction and when you have no preset idea of how it should work. Through my involvement with the conference, I learned so much from just being in that presence. Because I chose to sing with the Azusa Mass Choir, I was able to sit near the guest preachers and had the opportunity to soak up everything I heard. I couldn't get enough of what I was receiving; every inspiring message was working to rebuild me from the inside out. I felt it, I received it, I sat with it, and I owned every night of the conference.

When the conference ended, Higher Dimensions resumed its normal services on Sundays and Wednesdays. I was soon given the opportunity to audition to become a permanent member of the Higher Dimensions Choir. In the little country church where I grew up, I'd never heard of auditioning for a church choir before. At Higher D, however, this was how they determined if you had the minimum vocal skills necessary to become a member. So like everyone else before me, that's what I did. I was nervous and somewhat intimidated by all the beautiful voices that surrounded me. It seemed like every person in the choir was a professional singer, or at least they thought they were. I auditioned and continued going to rehearsals but didn't receive official notification that I had passed the audition for nearly three weeks.

No one voiced any objection to my membership in the choir; yet, not everyone was receptive to me joining, and there were moments when I felt less than completely welcome. The Higher D choir was an internationally famous, elite group, and it wasn't hard to pick up on the cold attitudes that some of the old guard members had toward me, an outsider and a newcomer. Nevertheless, there were others who were delighted that I was there. Regardless of how I was received, there was no turning back for me. There was a newness in my spirit and I knew I was in the right place at the right time for the right reasons. There was nothing that could stop me from pushing through to the next level.

I sat in the choir stand on the same platform behind Bishop Pearson every Sunday and Wednesday. I observed Gina each Sunday as she entered the sanctuary to take her reserved seat. Rarely did I interact with either of them. I watched them from afar mostly, always thinking how tired they must get of people sometimes. It seemed at every turn they made, there was someone right there with a need or conversation or question.

After services dismissed, sometimes I would watch Bishop Pearson literally stand in one spot an hour or more at a time, greeting everyone in line to shake his hand. He never knew what was in their minds, or on their hearts, or in their hands even. Sometimes it was hard to tell the sane from the insane. We never knew if the guests standing in line to greet him were happy to see him or angry that he existed. But for the most part, people just wanted a hello, a handshake, a touch, or an opportunity for him to speak into their lives. There was something magnetic about him that went far beyond celebrity status. Bishop Pearson had a way of making each individual feel like they were the only person that mattered in that moment. Somehow, just by being in his presence, you could feel the same wonderful energy that flowed through him, flowing in you.

Every single Sunday, I grew spiritually like a weed! I couldn't wait for Sunday to come around and hear what

Bishop Pearson would teach on next, or to hear him continue his message from the week before. It seemed that I was living exactly what he was teaching, so every message was healing for me; every Sunday, I left the building filled with enough life and enthusiasm to last my entire week. I was delighted to be the light in the office at work. On occasions, I would share what I was experiencing with others. The more I talked about what was going on inside of me, the more I would evolve. So many times, I wanted to share my story with Bishop Pearson. I wanted to let him know just how his words were affecting me. It was hard to get to him and have a conversation back in those days. He was always surrounded by long lines of people waiting to speak to him once the service ended. Because the wait was too long, I never did. In fact, perhaps a year or more passed before I actually spoke to him directly.

I felt no urgency to do so because even from a distance I was getting exactly the healing I needed. My interest was more in getting to know his parents, who were also regular attendees at Higher Dimensions. Adam and Lillie Pearson, affectionately known as "Mom" and "Dad" Pearson, were as warm and welcoming as you could possibly imagine. They were like the grandparents of the entire Higher Dimensions ministry. I was delighted to make their acquaintance. Having lost both of my parents, I can remember thinking how lucky Bishop Pearson was to still have them both alive and well and by his side every Sunday. They always entered the sanctuary smiling, waving, and greeting those in their path. They were usually accompanied by someone who had been assigned to assist them for the day. Mother Pearson was always beautifully dressed in the most stylishly accessorized dresses and beautiful suits. Whether she wore her hair flowing down, or pinned in an "up-do," she always looked so elegant and queenly to me. I don't know one woman in that church who would have disagreed. She continues to be a stunningly beautiful woman to this day. Dad Pearson was always right by her side, smiling, waving, blowing kisses, and hugging everybody within his reach. Although he was a gentle spirit, he was sharp-witted and never without a clever saying or two. One of my favorite sayings of his was, "I love ya and I like ya too!" To me, that covered it all. You could always tell how proud they were of their son and his accomplishments, of course, and it was a well-known fact that Bishop Pearson was proud of his parents. It was good to know and see where our leader came from and who had influenced him along the way.

I fastened myself into this ministry hook, line, and sinker. Based upon my own instinct and experience, I trusted everything about it and about Carlton Pearson. I got the distinct sense from some people that they thought I wasn't qualified to be there. Yet, I loved what I was learning, and I loved that I was understanding how to understand myself. I loved how open and transparent Bishop Pearson was. I loved how strong I was becoming, and I loved how his teachings resonated with the way my parents raised me to think and navigate through life in general. I did nothing but heal and evolve in this place. I was certain that everyone else was doing the same.

Bishop Pearson would tell stories of his Pentecostal upbringing. Many of the members could relate because they came from the same background. Although my family went to church religiously every Sunday, my background was very different. I didn't come from a Pentecostal upbringing. I was from a Baptist church and, compared to Pentecostals, the rules were a lot more liberal. But the church never regulated our lives; it was my parents who laid down the law in our home. The church was a backdrop and its authority was secondary to what my parents taught us. My mother spent her time living and teaching the morals of the Bible stories we heard. She emphasized how we should treat and get along with each other as siblings, as she was raising fourteen very different personalities. We heard and knew the Bible stories and studied them during Sunday School, but she drove home the meaning of those stories in her own way.

So, never having been a Bible scholar or a Bible student outside of the little country church where I came from, it never occurred to me to fact-check anything Carlton Pearson was teaching. This would not have been my inclination anyway, since I'd been taught to put everything into perspective for myself, and I did. To this day, there has been nothing said or taught that has been beyond possibility, according to my perception of God. It was working for me.

It was healing me. It saved my life. That's all that mattered.

Year after year, service after service, rehearsal after rehearsal, speaker after speaker, and Azusa after Azusa, it became non-stop purging and non-stop growth for me. I welcomed every drop of it.

CHAPTER 6

"The air stood still."

-Teresa

I t was on a Sunday morning, sometime late in the year 2000, when we anticipated one of those glorious services that only happened at Higher D. As always, the crowds had come with the usual excitement and anticipation. From floor to balcony, the sanctuary was a busy burst of color, and all of its seats were filled with beautiful, multi-ethnic people, most in their finest dress. The electrifying time of praise and worship was over, and the offering was taken. The visitors were acknowledged, and the choir had finished its soul-stirring selection under Pastor Jesse's direction. It was now time to hear Pastor Carlton share the Word of God as only he could.

The Word of God. Now, there's a common Evangelical expression. Like Pastor Carlton, I grew up Pentecostal, and my roots were in the Church of God in Christ. All my life, I had taken for granted that anything that was written in the

Bible was the *Word of God*—literally, a holy message directly from the Almighty Himself. I had also taken for granted that anything spoken by the preacher from the pulpit—with the Bible as its basis, of course—was the *Word of God*. From religious roots that extended, for me, back to toddlerhood, these were axioms, unshakeable, self-evident truths. No one ever questioned whether the Bible was the Word of God, and no one ever doubted that the preacher's role was to deliver the Word of God. Furthermore, no one ever doubted that the preacher was the Man of God whose job was to convey the Word of God. The Man of God, the Word of God—these axioms were truths as fixed in our collective conscience as two plus two equal four.

In most Christian homes—and certainly, in nearly every Black Christian home—the assumption that the Bible is synonymous with the *Word of God* is clearly evident. We record our births, deaths, and marriages in our Bibles. When loved ones die, we press their funeral flowers between its hallowed pages. We keep Bibles in places of reverence and honor in our homes. We believe it to be flawless, infallible, even somewhat magical.

I remember sitting in the choir stand with my perfect view of the congregation on that particular Sunday, when Pastor Carlton dared to raise a seismic question. His tone was different that day. He was pensive and contemplative as he approached the holy lectern that Sunday, lost in some unknown thought that he was about to unveil. What he offered that day was not the usual winning recipe of humor and fiery inspiration, but a series of questions, some of them unsettling. He was about to broach a subject that would immediately challenge one of our commonly-held assumptions about the Word of God. The congregation was attentive, quiet, and restless. None of us were entirely sure where he was going with his line of reasoning, but I leaned in. The title of his sermon that day was *Jesus, Savior of the World,* which was perfectly acceptable, as nobody had any doubts that Jesus was, indeed, Savior. But the culminating question he raised was one that veered from the well-worn path of familiar doctrine, time-honored axiom, and our religious tradition. He quoted II Corinthians 5:19 (KJV):

> *"To wit, that God was in Christ, reconciling the world unto himself, not imputing their trespasses unto them; and hath committed unto us the word of reconciliation."*

And then he spoke these words, posing a question that none of us ever expected to hear within the walls of Higher D: *"What if no one goes to hell?"* he asked. *"What if everyone is saved, but they just don't know it?"*

The air stood still. The body language in the congregation shifted from divine assurance to a mixture of sudden discomfort and intrigue, some of the congregants visibly appalled at his very suggestion. Others were impatient, eager to leave this cognitive uncertainty and get back to the familiar, feel-good part of the church experience that we all enjoyed. Perhaps some were disappointed that hell might be rendered useless; perhaps others were offended that Pastor Carlton had underscored what appeared to be a clear self-contradiction within the presumably infallible Word of God. Although I observed the congregation's reaction, I was most keenly aware of my own response. Pastor Carlton seemed to have found a scriptural basis for the possibility that nobody goes to hell. For me, this sparked an internal spiritual revolution, one that sent me on an investigative venture like no other. *Could it be true?*

The belief in hell was a part of my religious heritage, so I accepted it without question. But as much as I'd always looked forward to going to church, hell terrified me—its horrors having been described to me in graphic, gory detail from the time I was a very young child. I learned that hell was extremely hot, very dark, and that there were screams and cries from the tormented, who kept falling, falling, falling for all of eternity because it was a bottomless pit. By the time I was as young as five or six years old, preachers had already imprinted gruesome images of the demonic tortures of hell upon my young mind. Once in hell, there could be no escape.

As a young child, I suffered many sleepless nights due to nightmares about hell. Worst of all, for me, was the thought of anyone I loved going there. My father, for example, was never a Christian in the sense that we defined it. He smoked. He drank. He lost his temper and used foul language from time to time. But he was my hero, completely lovable, a caring and devoted husband to our mother, and an excellent and protective father. My sisters and I adored him. Daddy was a compassionate, generous, and sincere man despite his share of flaws. Under no circumstances could I ever imagine my father burning in hell for one moment, much less for eternity. And although my religious tradition said that he was headed to hell, the very thought of this was something I had no ability to digest. I reconciled my love for Daddy with my belief in hell by convincing myself that someday, somehow, Daddy would get "saved." In this way, I could hold onto both Daddy and hell. But it was 2000, and I was a grown woman, still believing in salvation, and hell, and the whole bit, as good Evangelicals were expected to do. And my dad, whom I still adored, had not yet recited the "Sinner's Prayer."

I couldn't imagine anyone, really, burning and suffering that way for all of eternity. Yet, our church taught—and I believed, as it was my duty to believe—that hell was real. In fact, in our theology, hell was almost every bit as necessary as God. If my church's teachings were to be taken seriously, most of my classmates, my neighbors, my teachers, my grandparents, aunts, uncles, cousins, and my Dad were destined for eternal torture. The Brady Bunch, the Jackson Five, the Partridge Family, Mary Tyler Moore, Carol Burnett, and the President of the United States were all going to hell. And they were going to hell at the hands of a loving God.

This cognitive dissonance—the tension between the teachings I embraced and the intuition that I sensed—occupied the hidden regions of my spiritual awareness for years. I grew up with it, went through high school and college with it, earned three degrees with it, and started my career with it.

Once I'd moved to Tulsa and joined Higher D, I was well practiced at ignoring the cognitive dissonance. I silently embraced what I knew was a ridiculous hope—that someday, somehow, most people about whom I cared would recite the "Sinner's Prayer," would adopt my precise collection of Evangelical beliefs, and thus, save themselves from eternal damnation. From time to time, however, I was driven by guilt to question the authenticity of my own convictions. If hell was a real danger to unbelievers, why wasn't I more urgently about the business of converting sinners? Why didn't I spend more time pleading with those I loved to turn from their wicked ways? If I really cared about them, how could I really resign myself to only hoping that someday they would come around to the soul-saving truth? Weren't the stakes too high to leave this to chance?

This occasional guilt would compel me to sell my beliefs to those who were about as interested in being converted as they were in having a root canal or buying "a lemon" of an automobile. Good Evangelical Christians, after all, were expected to evangelize, to get out there and proselytize, share the Good News, and save souls. I was always taught that the Scriptures commanded that I win souls to Christ.

During the course of my upbringing, I heard many fiery sermons about the soul-winning mandate, even to the point of quantifying how many people I should reach and convert within a given time period. I was taught, for example, that unless I was witnessing to sinners at least every week, I wasn't doing my job as a Christian. So, in a guilt-ridden, half-hearted, and perfunctory way, I found myself, on a few awkward occasions, striking up the "eternity" conversation. And it always felt scripted, fake, and inauthentic. I hated it.

By contrast, I always loved sharing about God's work in my life, about my sense of God's presence, about the incredible peace I got from praise and meditation, and my experience with answered prayers. These kinds of conversations were easy, genuine, and natural for me, and I could speak to anyone, anytime, anywhere about my own personal, spiritual journey. But attempting to convert people to my religion always felt self-aggrandizing, presumptuous, and wrong. These were feelings I kept to myself.

There were plenty of others, however, who were absolutely driven to evangelize and convert the world, eager to argue that our way was the only way to God. Higher D, in fact, was originally named Higher Dimensions Evangelistic Center, and its founding mission in the early 1980s was deeply grounded in this soul-saving mandate. In Evangelical speak, we often referred to "harvesting" souls as though they were these ethereal things you could collect. The motive for harvesting souls was to save them from hell by making them into

Christians. Our ironclad belief in hell was at the basis of the oft-repeated question intended to persuade sinners to change: "If you die tonight, do you know where you'll spend eternity?" we'd ask. Of course, the grand irony of believing so strongly in hell is the twisted comfort one takes in the thought that those who reject your beliefs will, well, end up in hell anyway.

And then, on that particular Sunday morning in 2000, quoting II Corinthians 5:19, Pastor Carlton had the audacity to ask: "*What if no one goes to hell? What if everyone is saved, but they just don't know it?*"

What if God's love is stronger than hell? The very thought of this was perhaps even more intriguing to James than it was to me. When he was a boy, his father committed suicide. After the loss of his business and eviction from their home, his father fell into a deep and hopeless depression. It was 1967, and there was simply no awareness that depression was a disease that could be treated. Instead, mental illness was highly stigmatized. People in that day didn't know that mental illness was often rooted in chemical imbalance and could be hereditary. Especially in the black community, there was no way to confront or address it. They simply suffered in shame and silence. For too many, death seemed the only way out of this misery.

At eight years old, James was awakened one morning by the sound of gunfire. He heard his mother scream, and the house was soon filled with paramedics and police officers.

His father lingered for several weeks before he died in a Veteran's hospital. James remembers getting a new suit for the funeral at Jack's Memory Chapel, and he remembers becoming the man of the house while still in elementary school.

Although his mother's side of the family was Catholic, James's uncle, a deacon in the Baptist church, took him under his wing and became, for him, a surrogate father. Over the years, as he attended the Baptist church, he heard that suicide was murder, and therefore, a sin displeasing to God. James was told that his father, who he loved and sorely missed, was guilty of suicide and, therefore, was in hell. Religious people, serving a loving God, told a grief-stricken little boy that his father was burning in hell.

No one can possibly understand the overwhelming and profound impact of depression without living through it. I certainly had no clue of what depression really was until March 1997, when James himself fell into a depression that nearly turned our world upside down. We hadn't been married quite a year when James got news that the office where he worked at Southwestern Bell (later, AT&T) was reorganizing. He would be transferred to a different location in the city where his department would combine with another one. In a period of corporate downsizing, neither of us thought this was a big deal; we were just grateful that he had accrued enough seniority by that time to keep his job.

His first day in the new location was March 3, 1997. He got

up that morning, got dressed, and had breakfast as usual. We kissed each other a cheerful goodbye and he left for work just like any other normal day.

But when he returned home that evening, my husband had become someone I didn't recognize. To make a long story short, the effect of the reorganization was more profound than he had anticipated. The changes were such that what James experienced was, in effect, a demotion. He felt as though the respect he'd earned, after seventeen years with the company, was suddenly irrelevant. This blow unleashed a well of emotion that James had managed to suppress since becoming the man of the house at eight years old.

At first, I thought James was just sad and would adjust and get over it in a couple of days. How wrong I was! What I didn't realize was that my husband had been holding it together all those years since his father's suicide, something with which he'd never fully dealt. The change on his job was just the trigger that unleashed thirty years' worth of festering grief and pain.

In my naivety, I encouraged him that things would get better and pushed him out the door to face a job he now hated. For the next three or four days, he dragged himself to work, but was like a zombie. Within a week, he simply refused to go, and began sleeping for hours, sometimes staying in bed for days at a time. He stopped eating, bathing, shaving and living. He just slept and stared off into space, and nothing I did—not my screaming, yelling, cursing, or threatening—made any difference. This was more than just sadness. It was a complete personality change, something that I'd never witnessed before.

He lost weight rapidly, and his emaciated and unshaven appearance further convinced him to barricade himself inside our home with no outside contact for weeks at a time. The thinner he got and the longer his hair grew, the more ashamed he was of his unkempt appearance, and the more fearful he was of facing the outside world. He slept all the time. When he was awake, he was engulfed in this thick cloud of gloom that was impossible to pierce. My love seemed to have no effect on him. This was bigger than me.

I took James to Laureate, a local psychiatric hospital. He was admitted, diagnosed with clinical depression, given some medication and a series of pep talks, and released after just a few days. Soon, he was back to the same routine of self-starvation and constant sleeping, and I was back to the same, exhausting routine of trying to push, cajole, persuade, and convince him to start living. But, he did not want to live. Something in his mind had malfunctioned, triggering inside of him the will to do nothing but self-destruct.

One day, I came into our bathroom where I found James unscrewing the cap off a bottle of Lysol. He had turned the bottle up, put it to his lips, and was preparing to drink it. This sight sent shots of horror through my entire body. I grew cold, numb, terrified, and enraged. We were still newlyweds; this wasn't supposed to be happening. I screamed and snatched the bottle from him and immediately proceeded to call 911. Within minutes, an ambulance, a fire truck, and a squad car, all with flashing lights, were parked outside of our home, a scene that announced our pain to the world. Our secret was out, as the spectacle attracted the attention of curious neighbors. James felt angry and invaded and accused me of overreacting. But I couldn't help but think of his father who had taken his own life thirty years before. I was willing to do whatever it took to keep history from repeating itself. I loved him.

This time, the police escorted James to Laureate, where he was admitted on an inpatient basis for a much longer time. Over the next two years, that hospital stay was followed by more relapses and more hospital stays. Meanwhile, I communicated with doctors, the insurance company, and with the union at his job on his behalf. I prayed that he would not be fired, hoping that his seventeen-year track record would somehow make up for his many days of missed work. Eventually, grace ran out and James was fired. Even worse was the day that I asked the doctor if I would ever get my husband back. His answer was, "I don't know. We've done all that we can do."

For two years, I was caught between my husband's severe battle with depression and the demands of my own new job. Nobody at the university had any clue that this was happening in my home. My husband was disappearing, our marriage was in shreds, and I was drained and exhausted;

however, I worked hard to appear cheerful and normal, to never let on. At church, I only told my closest friend, Kim, and our minister of music, Pastor David Smith. Along with his wife, Evangeline, Pastor David prayed with me for James to recover. My real strength, however, came from those times when I could steal away into a quiet place and lay on my face before God, pouring out my heart to Him, crying, heaving, loud and uncontrollably, allowing tears and snot and sweat to stain everything I thought I was. If my Pentecostal upbringing had taught me anything, it taught me how to leave my reality and to fervently pray myself into that trancelike state where God's incomprehensible peace is found. For two years, I had to do this on a regular basis. I needed God to keep James from killing himself, to keep me from killing James, and to help us both find our way back again.

It was a long, slow process. I vacillated between bouts of doubt and moments of hope, relying on the peace and comfort of prayer to uphold and renew me. Thankfully, miraculously, James did recover. Over time, he started to live again, and, for every day since, each time I've seen him smile has been worth more to me than all the gold in the world. But that experience left me both enlightened and humbled. It crushed every naive or judgmental assumption I may have ever had before about anyone driven to take his or her own life.

Depression is a serious, personality-altering disease that requires medication and professional help. Those who are suffering from depression make decisions, not rooted in sound judgement, but in a desperate effort to remedy an internal pain that is impossible for most people to comprehend. It is far more than a sadness you just "get over," and if left untreated, it can be fatal, as was the case with the father-in-law I never got a chance to meet.

During the period of his recovery, James heard Pastor Carlton say something that challenged the assertion that his father, because of the suicide, was burning in hell: "God may not call everyone home," he said tenderly. "But he welcomes them all home." Pastor Carlton then proceeded to describe a loving father, excited to embrace that dear one with outstretched arms and the firmest, healing embrace. As I heard Pastor Carlton address suicide in this way, I could literally see the love of God pouring into the self-inflicted gunshot wound in my deceased father-in-law's head. This image of a compassionate and welcoming God was the one that should have been conveyed to my husband when he was a hurting little boy.

And now, Pastor Carlton was issuing another challenge to the dogma that had so long defined our faith: *"What if no one goes to hell?"* he asked. *"What if everyone is saved, but they just don't know it? What if God's love is stronger than hell?"*

Sunday mornings at Higher D had always been exciting and inspiring but predictable. Electrifying praise, inspiring music, a rousing sermon, an offering, an altar call, a closing prayer, and an affirming benediction had always been as dependable as the earth's rotation around the sun. But not that particular Sunday. Pastor Carlton had started down a new and unfamiliar path. We all left church that day, not rejoicing, but questioning.

CHAPTER 7

"There was a restlessness that drove Bishop Pearson..."

— Cassandra

The country church that I attended while growing up had no celebrity pastors. Instead, our pastor was an ordinary person who was hired to preach. The real spiritual authority in our family came from our parents. As I became more familiar with the larger urban Black Church, I came to realize how much these pastors were regarded with a sense of affection and devotion, as well as with a certain degree of ownership. These pastors, it seemed, belonged to the people.

Church people love and respect their ministers, but they can tend to expect a lot from them. They expect that the minister's good reputation will be reflected in both his deeds and his personal presentation. They expect him to dress well and to have an admirable mode of transportation. They expect him to deliver on Sundays, to make the congregation feel more inspired and validated than when they first arrived to the service. The black pastor, in particular, is often viewed as the congregation's representative of Jesus, and, as such, he should be accessible and available to help his members navigate life's challenges. He is expected to be there to welcome babies, to baptize converts, to marry couples, to visit the sick, and to eulogize the deceased. His presence is also expected at revivals, at community events, and at celebrations of many kinds. By and large, black congregations expect that their pastors will keep and reinforce traditions, bringing to his role a unique spin on what is customary and expected. He is viewed as a father figure, a wise shepherd whose primary responsibility is to his own flock within the four walls of his own church. Black pastors who stray from tradition often meet with pushback.

Bishop Pearson had always been a bridge-builder. Although he himself was unapologetically black, Higher D was never an exclusively black church. Instead, from its very beginning, its congregation and ministerial staff were multiracial. Just as Higher D never quite fit into the traditional "black-church" mold, Bishop Pearson always defied the limitations of the traditional pastor's role. While he performed all of the ceremonial functions related to birth, marriage, death, and the like, there was no way that he, alone, could address the needs of a congregation six thousand strong. For needs of this sort, he was assisted by Higher D's large ministerial staff.

Even with a congregation this large, the gaze of Higher D always reached beyond the needs of its own membership. The church ran a food pantry called "The Raven's Nest" that provided assistance to families in the community in need of help. It sponsored an adoption agency, Hannah's Prayer, that placed the children of unwed mothers with qualified families. On the Higher D grounds were a credit union and a daycare, also open to the community. Bishop Pearson was a regular visitor to prisons in the Oklahoma region, bringing along the choir and the band to conduct full church services for those incarcerated.

His impact was never fully restricted to his church membership or even to the state of Oklahoma. He was a regular on Christian television and also had a following among secular viewers. Long before the year 2000, he had already met with presidents, and was being called upon to comment on current events. In April 1995, for example, he was on the program, along with President Bill Clinton, at a nationally televised service following the Oklahoma City bombing. There was a restlessness that drove Bishop Pearson to seek connections beyond his familiar circle.

His brief foray into politics was probably an expression of this restlessness. Bishop Pearson's inclusive thinking informed his vision for the city and prompted his decision to run for mayor of Tulsa. To many people, this announcement was a surprise, but it was common to hear him allude to taking ministry outside the four walls of the church. When he actually made the announcement to run, however, like many others at Higher Dimensions, I wasn't sure what to think at that time. I didn't know what it would mean for our church for him to win the election. Bishop Pearson's heart was always for the people, and I felt his purpose was to lead the people to their purpose. I knew that his messages had brought healing to me, and it was not hard for me to imagine his influence bringing healing to the city of Tulsa, with its deep racial divisions. Reaching higher and stretching further was something we watched him do many times, so supporting another one of his visions did not seem unreasonable.

In an interview with the *Tulsa World* on Oct 13, 2001, Bishop Pearson said, "My feeling is that Tulsa should be a twenty-first-century model city in all aspects, including race relations, economic development, education, city government and infrastructure."[1] He was persistent on the inclusiveness of God to work in every aspect of life. "One Tulsa" was his campaign slogan.

On October 16, 2001, Bishop Pearson officially tossed his hat into the ring to run as the first Republican, African American candidate for the mayor of Tulsa. It's important to note that Republicans in 2001 were very different in their message than they are today, in 2018. As of this writing, the Republican party has largely gone the unfortunate way of Donald Trump. When Bishop Pearson ran as a Republican in 2001, however, the party was most committed to a message of Christian values. And since blacks were underrepresented in the Republican party, he felt that his mayoral run was an opportunity to change that.

Just how would he make ministry and politics work together? That question became so intriguing to me that I signed up to help work the campaign. I believed that if anybody could make the two worlds complement each other, he was just the man to do it. The campaign process was a real eye-opener. The campaign gave me an opportunity to watch Bishop Pearson operate as "Carlton Pearson" outside of his normal religious arena. "One Tulsa" was his slogan, and making it the gathering place was his mission. The interviews, the press conferences, and the debates left me in awe of the amount of information one individual could absorb and retain. There was no doubt in my mind that he was highly capable of leading in any profession he chose. I often wondered what other profession he might have chosen had he not chosen ministry.

But as fate and the city of Tulsa would have it, in February 2002, Bishop Pearson lost the primary election to his Republican opponent, and native Tulsan, Bill LaFortune. The LaFortunes are well-known Tulsa conservatives, a generous family that has contributed much to the city, both in politics and philanthropy.

I can't say that I was disappointed that Bishop Pearson lost the election; politics was uncharted territory for him and campaigning was grueling work. The truth is, I was elated to have his full attention back at Higher Dimensions Church.

1. Lassek, P.J. "Carlton Pearson to Run for Mayor." *Tulsa World*, October 31, 2001.

CHAPTER 8

"The exodus from Higher D began as a trickle..."

-Teresa

James and I leaned into what Pastor Carlton was saying about the inclusive work of the Cross. There—in Scripture—appeared to be as strong an argument for the mercy of God as for the wrath of God. His sermons triggered a flood of thoughts and questions, awakening and exposing the cognitive dissonance between my inherited beliefs and the intuition about God that I'd had all my life. I knew God as Savior, Keeper, Deliverer, the Almighty whose mercies are new each morning and whose love is everlasting. From childhood, I'd known of Psalm 139:8 (KJV), the verse that says:

> *If I ascend up into heaven, thou art there.*
> *If I make my bed in hell, behold thou art there.*

As this verse suggests, my intuition had always been that God's mercy overrules hell. My religious tradition, on the other hand, taught powerfully and emphatically that hell overruled God's mercy. Pastor Carlton was inviting me to safely consider the possibility that maybe—just maybe—my religious tradition had gotten it wrong. Maybe I could finally erase that troubling image of my father, grandfather, aunts, uncles, cousins, and most of Africa, Asia, and Europe being tossed around in the flames of damnation for all of eternity.

While I and a few others leaned in, many more—thousands more, actually—were appalled at Pastor Carlton's audacity. Tampering with hell was like removing the one screw that held the entire Evangelical machine together. Jesus giving His life was nice and all, but hell was the *real* incentive for salvation. Invariably, his opponents pointed to the sanctity and infallibility of scripture to prove the reality, indeed, the indispensability of hell. Simultaneously, Pastor Carlton pointed to scripture from the same Bible to argue for the infallibility of God's love.

I had been steeped in Evangelical Christian thought my entire life, so I knew well the high premium placed on spiritual superiority. From childhood, mine had been a decidedly fundamentalist paradigm juxtaposing "us" and "them", "the church," and "the world." We were separatists through and through—polite and cordial, but separatists, nonetheless. I'd grown up in the sanctified church, wearing dresses in the dead of winter, getting religious excuses every year from attending gym classes, all because my church taught me that I was required to be noticeably distinct from the world. To be sure, my strict church upbringing gave me many precious gifts that I still treasure to this day. But it taught me, just as powerfully, that my church's truth was the only truth, that my church's road to salvation was the only way; any departure from this truth, from this way, was to be thoroughly, completely, immediately, and summarily rejected. So I understood why the members of Higher D began to scatter. Yet, it hurt. It was a deep, cutting, and unforeseen pain.

In the black church, when the pastor preaches, you answer back. This is the culture. The preacher makes a statement, and if you feel in tune with what is being said, you shout "Amen!" Traditionally, black church services are dialogues, so there is never a moment when you have to guess whether or how the sermon is being received. For me, Pastor Carlton's questions were intriguing. His deep dive into scripture—not repeating the familiar spin, but looking carefully and critically at what was actually there—awakened and inspired the scholar in me. I was thirsty, almost desperate to know more, and I didn't keep it a secret. But it wasn't enough for me to blindly accept what he was suggesting; I had to do my own research and wrestle internally with my long-held beliefs. I was enthusiastic about examining credible sources, about learning new truths. The more digging I did, the more evidence I found that Pastor Carlton was onto something. I was beginning to see the power of God and the incredibly far reach of God's love in a whole new way. In my own study, I found evidence to support Pastor Carlton in his quest. During church services, while many others squirmed in discomfort, my "Amens!" made clear my support of his doctrinal shift. The consequence, however, was that I was soon branded one of *them.*

The exodus from Higher D began as a trickle at first. From our vantage point in the choir stand, we could see the body language and facial expressions of people hoping that this was just some crazy phase, midlife crisis perhaps. Pastor Carlton would certainly get through this, get over himself, and get back to entertaining and uplifting the crowds as he always had. On Sunday mornings, the sanctuary had always been full of arms raised with hands uplifted in prayer and praise. Now, many had their arms tightly and defensively folded across their chests, their faces clearly impatient with this ridiculous talk of Jesus saving the whole world and nobody going to hell.

Mother's Day was usually one of the more elaborate Sunday morning services, as we always had a tradition of honoring mothers who had achieved certain milestones. In the black church, it is the custom to give special flowers to the oldest mother, the newest mother, the mother with the most children, etc. By Mother's Day 2002, the sanctuary still appeared mostly full; certain key members of the church, however, were conspicuously absent. As I sat in the choir stand during the Mother's Day tributes, another one of the sopranos sitting beside me leaned over to whisper in my ear. Joyce had been a popular song leader, a staple in the soprano section, and a regular voice on the Azusa recordings. Over the years, we'd been in countless rehearsals together, and although we weren't bosom buddies, I did consider her a friend.

She leaned over to whisper to me: "I just want you to know that this is my last Sunday at Higher D," she said. "The Lord is showing me that it's time to move on." We were in the middle of Sunday service and there was no space at that moment to have a conversation about it. I smiled and wished her well, saddened that our choir would be without her and her talents. She stayed until the benediction that day but was true to her word; she left the church and I never saw her at Higher D again.

As the weeks and months wore on, the congregation, bit by bit, continued to thin. And God was speaking to many others, telling them to flee from Higher Dimensions and from Pastor Carlton, who was now considered by many to be a False Prophet. (I capitalize "False Prophet" because, in our tradition, such persons are to be feared, condemned, and shunned.) I was at Albertson's, the neighborhood grocery store, where it was common to bump into others who lived in the area. It was especially awkward, however, to run into someone who once had been a regular at Higher D, but who had been away for some weeks or months now. A clear line of division had already formed, with true keepers of the faith on one side and those of us who had been deceived and led astray by Carlton Pearson on the other.

I was at the store to buy chicken wings for dinner one night when I ran into another choir member—another song leader—whose absence from choir practice and church services had been conspicuous for several weeks. She was a strong personality and a popular Christian leader who was highly regarded by many. I placed my package of chicken wings in my shopping cart along with my other items and started in her direction. We smiled, greeted each other warmly, and exchanged hugs. She then asked what was becoming a routine question:

"So, where do you go to church now?" she asked.

Her question was loaded with the assumption that I, too, was certainly part of the righteous mass exodus. She was sure that I had left Higher D and was most likely worshipping elsewhere.

"I'm still at Higher D," I responded, instantly realizing that I had given the wrong answer.

Her facial expression changed. Right there, by the poultry section, she exhorted as though warning me of grave danger: "God told me to get out of there as fast as possible!" she exclaimed, emphatic enough to be heard a couple of aisles over. "He's preaching false doctrine!"

Her warning was emphatic and blunt, leaving me no space except to be someone deceived by false doctrine. I felt punched in the stomach. Quickly, I made up something about needing to get dinner done before James came home. I hurried to extract myself from the debate that she was seeking and that I refused to have.

There was a similar incident at another grocery store—this time, at Wild Oats, which later became Whole Foods. A man whose name I didn't know, but who knew of me from a distance because of my visibility in the choir, approached me as I was in the line to check out. Before even saying "hello," or asking my name, he began with, "Are you still at Higher D?" I answered that I was. He then started what he apparently intended to be a lengthy discourse, one that he seemed to have practiced in advance:

"Sister, the Scripture says . . . ." and he proceeded to quote to me Bible verses. I had heard these versus all my life and knew from memory, verses about sinners, and salvation, and hell and damnation. He sincerely believed that by repeating to me what I already knew, I would somehow return to my Evangelical senses and part ways with the False Prophet.

I don't remember how I extracted myself from that conversation, since he was still preaching to me as I was paying for my groceries and heading out the door. I only know that I somehow got away.

But the street where I lived was no safer than the supermarket. Pastor Carlton's break with the faith, his rejection of hell, was making news around the city. Christians from other churches were becoming concerned, and our neighbors three houses down made it their mission to confront us one day when we were out for a walk.

Vicki and Kevin Morris were a pleasant young couple and relatively new to the neighborhood. They were delightful, good Christian people who attended a different church across town. We typically exchanged pleasantries about the weather, our lawns, and our pets. Before that day, however, we had never had a conversation with them about anything more serious than this.

As we headed down the street for our walk, the two of them waved and approached us:

"Hey, guys, can we ask you a question?"

We answered "Sure," believing perhaps that it would be for advice on where to get the best fertilizer for fescue.

"Where do you go to church now?"

Again, the question was loaded with the assumption that we had fled like so many others. James and I looked at each other, suddenly getting an uneasy sense of where this was going.

"We still go to Higher D," we answered, much to their disappointment.

"What do you think about what Pastor Pearson is saying? About everyone being saved and no one going to hell?"

I responded that I was very interested in what he was saying and that it made a lot of sense to me.

"Oh, no!" Vicki exclaimed with urgency. "What you're doing is very dangerous, and you have to be careful. You can't . . . "

I cut her off mid-sentence, unwilling to spend another ten seconds in what was sure to not end well. I was shocked at the freedom, indeed the authority they felt to interrupt our walk in order to confront and scold us in this way. Their warning to us was dire and heartfelt. I understood their perspective because I'd been raised in it from birth. And yet, I was deeply offended at being cornered by people who felt it was their duty to correct and control our thinking.

I understood the good intentions behind each one of these encounters, and I believe they really felt duty-bound to try and save us. They were convinced that Carlton Pearson was going to hell and that he was leading us there, too; they felt they had to do something about it. The impulse they felt to correct us was in keeping with the Evangelical mandate to evangelize, to proselytize others, and to convert as many sinners as possible. I, myself, had always understood and accepted that it was my responsibility to lead others to Christ. Even when I was thoroughly Evangelical in every other way, however, I never felt comfortable with the dogmatic sales pitch. And now that I was on the receiving end of it, I understood why.

Joyce was the only person who mentioned to me her plans to leave the church. She didn't owe me that information; yet, I respected her for giving me fair warning so that I could adjust my expectations. It let me know that, on some level, she saw us as a family.

I was heartbroken to see my church family changing, shrinking, disappearing. A large part of that Sunday morning energy and spark of Higher D had been the huge crowd. It would have been impossible for any one person to get to know the thousands who attended there. The church was so big that it was common to never meet or even see those who sat apart from the section you typically chose. Yet, of those thousands, there were maybe a hundred or more people that I did know by name, people in the choir, or that I saw on Thursday evenings at Purity Class, or encountered at morning prayer or on Wednesday nights, or came to know more intimately because they also lived in the area where I lived or worked, or studied at the university where I taught. Of that hundred or so, there may have been about twenty that were in our closest circle, friends with whom we double-dated, or whose homes we visited, whose children we babysat; these were friends who invited us to cookouts, and who ate meals at our home; friends whose weddings we attended, whose baby showers, birthdays, anniversaries, and graduations we celebrated. These were friends who were welcome at our table and we at theirs on holidays throughout the year; friends we visited when they were sick, who visited us when we were sick, and with whom we shared grief when they were bereaved. We loved them, would have given them the shirts off our backs. And we believed they loved us, too.

Higher D was the center, the focus of our complex social network and its many different ties and connections. Coming together on a regular basis for church seemed the most important affirmation of these various relationships. Except for Joyce, every one of our friends who left Higher D did so quietly, without warning. The invitations to cookouts, to birthday parties, to graduations, to anniversaries, the friendly acknowledgements in passing, the occasional phone calls just to check in and say hello—that all just stopped. The silent disagreements between us were loud and burdensome. The chance encounters at the grocery store or in the mall became incredibly awkward; it was obvious when they pretended not to see us. It stung.

Having grown up in Evangelical Christianity, I understood perfectly well the need that people felt to escape Higher D and its dangerous, new theology. I am sure that many of our former friends felt a scriptural mandate to part company with us, as the Bible clearly warns of being "unequally yoked" with unbelievers. What baffles me to this day, however, is that there was no space for conversation. The only occasions on which I was engaged in any kind of exchange was to be told that I was wrong, had been deceived, and needed to repent and return to the fold. The script became almost predictable. First, I'd be asked where I attended church. Then, I'd be immediately castigated and rebuked for my misguided beliefs. At that point, I just felt battered and wanted to get away.

At no point was I ever asked—not even by my closest of friends—to explain why my views were changing. The assumption was that I was just a gullible sheep being led astray by Carlton Pearson. For sure, Pastor Carlton gave me permission to confront Biblical contradictions that had bugged me my entire life; I had arrived at plenty of my own reasons to conclude that the redemptive work of Christ was truly successful, and that no one would burn in hell. I came to these conclusions through study and research, but no one seemed interested in what I was learning on my own.

Over the years, I have often wondered whether those who left Higher D felt any pain at all in doing so. After all, we had been a family—thousands strong—but a family, nonetheless. I've wondered whether they ever experienced any sense of loss, any nostalgic longing for a return to the days when our thousands of multicolored voices sang, prayed, and worshipped together. I've wondered whether they've ever mourned over the disappearance of that something special in South Tulsa that we all shared. I've wondered whether, within the privacy of their own hearts, they've even entertained the possibility that maybe we weren't reprobates after all. I know about my sense of loss; I've tasted plenty of salt in my own tears. But I've wondered about their tears, if there were any at all.

Lillie Ruth and Adam (aka "Mom & Dad") Pearson

Pastor Carlton addressing the congregation
for the last time at Higher Dimensions
Family Church
8621 S. Memorial Drive

Photo courtesy of Doug Henderson,
Douglas Henderson Photography& Design
Tulsa, Oklahoma

Worshipping at Trinity Episcopal Church

Actress Lisa Bonet visits the New Dimensions congregation at Trinity Episcopal Church

The New Dimensions Choir on Sunday
morning at Trinity Episcopal Church

Pastor Carlton and members of New Dimensions Choir praying during rehearsal at Trinity Episcopal Church

Pastor Jesse at Barnes & Noble book-signing for *The Gospel of Inclusion*

James and Teresa Reed at Trinity
Episcopal Church

Cassandra attending a watch party on the evening of the 2008 presidential election

Carlton and Gina Pearson prior to their move to Chicago

Pastor David Smith leading worship at the keyboard at All Souls Unitarian Church

Marlin Lavanhar, Carlton Pearson, and
Joshua Marston at the Tulsa premiere
of *Come Sunday*,
April 8, 2018

CHAPTER 9

"In every empty seat, I saw the person who was once there."

-Teresa

The news that Pastor Carlton was preaching a strange, new doctrine spread like wildfire. It didn't take long for the Evangelical establishment to express its displeasure with what he was suggesting. Even with the ample backing of Scripture, church members and leaders alike found his challenge to their long-held beliefs to be not only offensive, but dangerous.

Our last Azusa Conference at the Mabee Center was in 2001. That year, Pastor Carlton invited noted gospel singer Gene Martin to appear with our choir; he was also featured on our recording, *Live at Azusa 4*, singing his stirring rendition of "Too Close to Heaven." Gene Martin was well known among older Pentecostals—black and white, alike—as the featured singer with A.A. Allen's tent revivals of the 1960s; yet, I'd never heard of him before. The invitation for him to appear at that Azusa was a deliberate effort on the part of Pastor Carlton both to bring this talented singer out of relative obscurity and to introduce him to a generation that knew nothing about him. With his booming, distinctive voice, Martin's appearance that year was particularly meaningful in another important way. He was sixty-two years old, and a pillar of the Pentecostal community. And, he had never married. He was never known to have ever fathered children. For as far back as I can remember, it had been whispered in black gospel circles that some of the most visible and talented singers and musicians in our choir stands and pulpits were same-gender-loving people. Yet, from these same pulpits come fire-and-brimstone sermons condemning homosexuality and damning gay people to hell. Evangelical Christianity has been completely schizophrenic where the LGBTQ community is concerned, greedily consuming their money-fetching artistic gifts on the one hand, but swiftly dismissing them as sinful and abnormal on the other. Pastor Carlton's bold decision to feature Gene Martin that year thus underscored yet another paradox in Evangelical thinking. His public and compassionate embrace of this largely-forgotten singer also signaled the heresy he'd begun to consistently preach. By this time, that heresy was nicknamed the "Gospel of Inclusion."

Five months later, on September 11, 2001, all eyes turned to the east. Our nation watched in horror as the World Trade towers fell at the hands of terrorists. It was a time of uncertainty as well as a paradigm shift in our national consciousness. As often as it replayed those scenes of horror, the media showed images of an unprecedented American unity. People of different faiths, ethnicities, nationalities, and gender identities came together in vigils large and small, forming a united front against bigotry and fear.

After several years at the Mabee Center, we had the 2002 Azusa Conference at the much smaller, older Tulsa Convention Center. For the first time in the history of the conference, there was a mysterious collection of coincidental cancellations. Well-known preachers and major artists, some of them Azusa regulars, backed out of their agreements to minister claiming illness, missed flights, or scheduling conflicts. Despite the fact that the conference had always been scheduled to occur at the same time every year, the supposed "last-minute" cancellations of so many preachers and artists seemed, at least to me, both coordinated and planned well in advance.

Although the Convention Center was smaller than the Mabee Center, there were still noticeable gaps in the audience. As anemic as the crowd was that year, we recorded an album, *Azusa Praise 2: We Cry Out* at the 2002 conference. The once-three-hundred-voice Azusa Mass Choir was diminished from what it had been in previous years. Yet, we prepared for this project with the same zeal and dedication that we'd given to earlier ones. As usual, we spent hours in rehearsals and recording sessions at the studio. Between takes, our typical lighthearted laughing and joking with each other was dampened by the conspicuous absence of singers who had been with us on every project before, but who were now gone. Under the expert direction of Pastor David Smith, we completed the project, and the recording was released in October 2002.

Our prior recordings had always been well-received, and were featured regularly on all of the major gospel music outlets. We expected no less from this recording, especially since the music was some of our best work. However, sales of *Azusa Praise 2: We Cry Out* completely failed to launch. The album was shipped around the country for distribution, but thousands of copies of the CD were returned to the record company, still in unopened boxes. By this time, the Evangelical establishment had convinced most of its churches that Carlton Pearson was a False Prophet, and that anything he produced was poisonous. Along with the rejection of *We Cry Out*, Carlton Pearson's music and the previous *Live at Azusa* and *Azusa Praise* recordings all but disappeared from the airwaves and from the shelves of Christian bookstores. Word had spread rapidly that Pastor Carlton was preaching another gospel, a different gospel, a dangerous gospel. Now, even his music—glorious songs of praise to a loving God— was tainted and suspect.

In 2003, we held our last conference in the Azusa tradition in our sanctuary at 8621 S. Memorial Drive. We no longer had the following or the resources to rent the big convention centers as we'd always done. March had always ushered in the first blooms of springtime along with the real start of Azusa season at the church. In years prior, it was always in March that the excitement became palpable, as we were well into rehearsals and preparations for the conference. That year, I tried to make the best of things. I imagined this conference (we still thought of it as "Azusa") to be a special gathering of our friends and family to our home rather than to some huge, rented auditorium. Higher Dimensions had always fronted the expense of Azusa, but this year, we would really be hosting the conference in the truest sense.

On the weekend preceding the conference, James and I spent the day at the church, cleaning, polishing, vacuuming, trying to feel some positive anticipation. We were becoming excited about the appearance of guests who, though fewer in number, would receive our warmest welcome, nonetheless. Some of the men from the church were busy mowing the lawn and putting finishing touches on the landscaping that faced Memorial Drive. Along with some of the ladies, I brought my own vacuum and cleaning supplies from home to help tidy up the church. Those of us who remained, remembering the glory days of Azusa, assumed that, even with a much smaller crowd, our church should be filled with visitors whose arrival we anxiously awaited.

Every year for more than the preceding decade, tens of thousands of people had flocked faithfully to Tulsa to attend Azusa in April. I did the math in my head. If even half of those people came for this year's conference, or even one third, then our auditorium at Higher D should be full. Our hearts longed to see the sanctuary full again.

Easter Sunday, which traditionally marked the start of our conference, came and went. There were no long lines, no crowds to be seen. The next day, Monday evening, was the official start of the series of night services. James and I dressed and got to the church early, certain that we would see both local and out-of-town visitors filing in. I recalled that just a few years earlier, the Azusa crowd began gathering outside of the Mabee Center by 4:00pm. A line a quarter-mile long usually formed in anticipation of the doors opening at 6:30. In rain or shine, hundreds stood waiting, sometimes singing, sometimes praying, or just happily chatting, anxious for the start of that glorious evening service.

In April 2003, things were very different. We waited. No line ever formed at the entrance. Finally, a few people started to arrive. I counted fewer than twenty visitors from out of town and fewer visitors than that from across town. Instead of the huge crowd, the excitement, and the anticipation, there was a mostly-empty building with ample available seating. Those of us who had prepared for the service faced the evening with a quiet sense of confusion and disappointment. At best, there were five hundred people in attendance. There was no one leading the 6:30pm prayer, and our choir—our Azusa Mass Choir—was barely thirty voices, with less than a handful of guests from other churches joining us. Most of the musicians were gone. Pastor David Smith was there, and

Chip Goines was there on drums. From our elevated vantage point in the choir stand behind the altar, we could see it all: a once-full auditorium sprinkled with empty seats and not even half-full. In every empty seat, I saw the person who was once there. I saw Paul and Marjorie, whose empty seats were in the far left section, two rows back near the aisle. I saw Grace and Phil, whose empty seats were in the first row near the center. I saw Ronda and Ken's empty seats, far left section, three rows back, just to the left of Paul and Marjorie. I saw Melvin and Diane's empty seats, Karen and Edward's empty seats, Mom and Dad Mason's empty seats, too many empty seats to count. I saw the seats where Shirley, Tina, Greg, Lisa, Brenda, Michelle, and Tameka all once sat, seats now empty and available for others to occupy, others who never came.

Church is as stable as a tree with roots a hundred miles deep, firmly planted by the ever-changing streams of life. Church is mother, father, and family. But our church, Higher D, was dying of empty seats, unspoken dissent, and the need to flee. Having questioned the sanctity of hell—indeed, the veracity of its existence—our once-celebrated church and its once-popular pastor had now become a leprous disease.

I learned an important lesson that year about change. Within the space of few years, the Azusa Conference, which had attracted as many as forty thousand people from around the world, had shrunk to a few hundred. It had gone from drawing the biggest names in Evangelical Christendom to attracting virtually no one at all. The decline was swift, dramatic, and severe. Big-name preachers and evangelists who had gotten their starts at Azusa, and who had once heaped public praise on Carlton Pearson, were suddenly nowhere to be found. Higher D, once the centerpiece of black Pentecostalism, was now branded, isolated, and ignored.

James and I didn't speak when we rode home that Monday night. The five minutes from South Memorial Drive to our house one street over on Mingo was the longest ride of our lives up until that point. We held hands but did not speak. We pulled into the garage, went into the house. James put down his keys, I dropped my purse on the counter. Then we both leaned against the center island in our kitchen, held each other, and we cried.

CHAPTER 10

"*I wanted to share my healing with others.*"

– Cassandra

Thank God, the dark cloud over my life was dissipating! Year after year, service after service, rehearsal after rehearsal, speaker after speaker, and Azusa after Azusa, it was non-stop purging and growth for me. I welcomed every drop of it. I took advantage of everything I could to further enhance who I was. With Higher D in transition and Bishop Pearson becoming more isolated, I didn't know what the future held; I just knew that my own recovery from paralyzing grief contained the seed of my next level. I recognized the fertile ground on which I stood.

Soon after joining the choir, it demanded a large chunk of my time each week, and it quickly became a priority. Everything else, outside of work, was scheduled around the time I spent singing and rehearsing. Our regular choir schedule included two (sometimes three) Sunday services, rehearsals on Tuesday evenings, and service on Wednesday evenings. During my early years with the choir, we also accepted countless special invitations to sing at other churches, at prisons, at community events, and at a variety of special functions. We accompanied Bishop Pearson on several occasions to both male and female prisons. With fire and compassion, he ministered to the inmates, some of whom included Higher D members, former members, and their spouses or children. We also accompanied him to little country churches in remote towns, as no venue was too small or insignificant for him to visit. Over the years, singing with the Higher D choir brought me into contact with people that I might have never otherwise met, and places that I might have never gone.

By the 1990s, the Higher D choir was known around the country, so my participation in it seemed larger than life. All the time I invested was restored to me in ways that money could never buy. Pastor Alvin Fruga was Higher D's Minister of Music when I joined in 1995. That same year, he was succeeded by Pastor David Smith, who continues to lead a chorale of former Higher D choir members to this day. To say the least, it was one of the greatest privileges of my life.

Bishop Pearson once told us that he didn't only study the Word of God, but he also studied words in general. He spent many hours researching, reading through dictionaries, encyclopedias, and scholarly books. I can remember thinking to myself, *Who does that?* Yet, his ability to shed light on the root meanings of words was one of the most captivating things about listening to his messages. There was a rich balance between his mastery of words, his explanations of scripture, and his own experiences with God. He also had a way of making his sermons connect to what was happening in the world. Thus, his messages were always current and relevant, and helped me to find my own place in what I already knew. Given that he was a scholar himself, it is no wonder that he decided to create a place where others could deepen their understanding about spiritual truths.

In 2000, Bishop Pearson opened the Azusa Christian Life School of Theology and I enrolled there as a part-time student. An interdenominational Christian college, the "Azusa School of Ministry," as we called it, was the Tulsa site of the Beacon College headquartered in Columbus, Georgia. Half of my classes were online, and the other half were taught on the church campus during the weekend. It seemed that I had travelled light years from the dark place that originally brought me to Higher D. I was hungry to learn more and eager to continue my own growth. I wanted to share my healing with others. The school was founded with the mission *to help people reach their God-given potential and equip them for His service.* There were courses of study offered in pastoral, counseling, evangelistic, teaching, music, youth and children's ministries. I jumped on board the Biblical Studies Program with an emphasis on Christian Counseling. I took several classes including *2000 Years of Charismatic History, The Theology of the Blood, A Study of Biblical Worship, The Kingdom of*

God, The Beatitudes, Old Testament Survey, New Testament Survey, The Life of Christ, and *Biblical Foundations of Counseling.*

Ironically, Bishop Pearson opened the school just around the same time he began to teach that Jesus was Savior of the world—the *entire* world. Unlike some preachers, he never spoke in a way that made me think he had an exclusive relationship with God. He always made me feel like God was accessible and present for anyone.

As he discussed God's inclusive love from the pulpit, I heard him think out loud as he remained open and vulnerable about something that was not yet fully formed in his own mind. This allowed me to understand that God permits this in all of us. I just assumed that we were all free to process our own questions and thoughts until we found a resolve within our own selves. I felt free to embrace my own interpretation of God. To me, the idea that God was accessible to everyone only reiterated what I'd already believed. I had no problem understanding what Bishop Pearson was trying to convey.

It took a good while before I realized, however, that there was a *fly in the buttermilk.* I suppose that if my church background had been the same as Bishop Pearson's, I would have noticed a shift in what he was teaching as quickly as others did, but I didn't. When I first came to Higher Dimensions, I was in so much pain that I had tunnel vision. I was only looking for my healing and that is exactly what I experienced. I dared not question what helped me survive that period. However, there was lots of background chatter.

I soon learned that there were church members who had become disgruntled about what he was now teaching, but I wasn't sure why. Since I had to be in my place to sing with the choir, I didn't have much time to mingle with the congregation after services and learn what all the fuss was about. But as Bishop Pearson continued to teach that Jesus was the Savior, not just of Christians, but of the whole world, things changed.

There I was thinking we were in the beginning of a massive love campaign, that we could now all celebrate God's inclusive love for all people. But I was wrong. Never, in my wildest dreams, did I think that people in church could consciously turn their backs and abruptly leave Higher D, nor did I ever think they would remain angry enough to distance themselves from us in the way that they did. Of all people, I assumed that church people were skilled in the art of getting along and working together despite their differences. I assumed that we could agree to disagree, and because of our history together, I really thought moving forward was possible.

The first time that I realized the extent of the controversy was on a Monday morning at my place of employment at the time. Having literally begun to live again, it was normal for me to bring the enthusiasm from a Sunday service to work with me on a Monday. This excitement and joy would carry me through my work week. Sometimes I would share parts of

Bishop Pearson's Sunday message with my co-workers, or I'd share what I was learning in my own relationship with God.

On this particular Monday morning, before the day had even gotten started, one of my co-workers who attended a different church across town came in the office and walked straight up to me and asked: "What is this shit I'm hearing about Carlton Pearson? Something about preaching there is no hell?"

She continued, "I like him a lot, and I wouldn't think he would be teaching something crazy, so that's why I'm coming to you. I figured you could tell me what's really going on."

She then proceeded to tell me that her minister informed their congregation that Carlton Pearson was erroneously telling everyone they were already saved. Her minister even played a snippet of an actual recorded sermon in which Carlton said he didn't believe in hell anymore. I couldn't understand why one preacher would feel such an urgency to publicly denounce another preacher for expressing a new point of view.

This workplace conversation caught me totally off guard. I was stunned. For the first time, it dawned on me that there may be real trouble for us, and for Carlton, in this town. I asked her if she could get a tape of her minister's sermon from that Sunday so I could hear it for myself. She did. The problem was not that he played the tape or mentioned Carlton's sermon to his congregation; the problem was that he played just enough to intentionally stir up controversy.

I knew right then that this would not be over soon enough.

It wasn't until after that incident when I began to notice that this had gone beyond our church. It seemed like the floodgates were opened. Talk got louder, articles were written, and more members were leaving. Outsiders were looking in, speculating and commenting about things they didn't know. Church people said things and wrote things about Carlton Pearson that were just downright mean, harsh, and hateful. It went from bad to worse. Attitudes changed toward our church within the city. There were businesses that no longer welcomed us or Bishop Pearson. Small business owners who continued to support Bishop Pearson were hit especially hard, as they lost clients because of this. Tulsa's largest Christian bookstore, which had previously carried Bishop Pearson's books and several years' worth of Azusa recordings, started to remove all products related to Higher D from the shelves of each of their three stores.

This censorship occurred in Christian markets around the country. Local religious radio stations no longer played Bishop Pearson's recordings on their programs. Nationally syndicated gospel radio, which had always played Bishop Pearson's music on a regular basis, swiftly removed his recordings from their rotations. People felt it was their job to isolate Higher Dimensions and to render the judgement of God.

During this time, Carlton was more than happy to answer questions and speak to anyone who wanted to talk to him;

everyone was welcomed. He had panel discussions and invited leaders to participate. Some came seeking understanding, others came to debate—using cherry-picked scriptures from the same Bible upon which the Gospel of Inclusion was based. Despite the vitriol constantly hurled at him, Carlton remained open to all who were concerned— much more open than I could have ever been—that's for sure! He seemed to be doing everything in his power to deescalate the growing controversy, and to make his critics understand what he was seeing. Nevertheless, he became more and more of an outcast. For Carlton, denying the truth in his spirit was evidently a greater risk than losing friendships. Sometimes, that's just the way it is in life. *Give me liberty or give me death* is real for some.

It was 2003. That year, the Joint College of African-American Pentecostal Bishops invited Bishop Pearson to their annual meeting to present his Gospel of Inclusion. This organization was founded by Bishop J. Delano Ellis, II and included the most elite and influential voices among black Evangelicals. Bishop Pearson travelled to the meeting, eager to share his teaching; he trusted that there was genuine interest in his message. After all, this organization included many people he'd known and worshipped with for years. So he welcomed the opportunity to engage in what he believed would be a dialogue with his peers. The dialogue, however, never happened.

The atmosphere was formal and austere, as the bishops, all

in their clergy attire, waited for Bishop Pearson to take the podium. He began his presentation by stating that he'd sent his position paper to several panelists and others in the College to review in advance. From that paper, Bishop Pearson began reading the following words:

> *The presentation I am about to submit to you is a work in progress. I have been working on and through the development of these thoughts and reflections for over twenty-five years and more openly and perhaps more progressively the last four or five. It is a work of faith and conviction, a mindset I've unsuccessfully tried to either avoid or delay fully accepting. This presentation is part of my witness and testimony as one who desires to both minister and worship as a citizen in the modern world and be able to think as I do so.*

Bishop Pearson's presentation continued for approximately forty-five minutes, ending with these powerful words:

> *I believe that we do have the message of reconciliation that can bring peace to this world ... but I wanted to tell you conceptually and comprehensively what I'm thinking. I've come to the conclusion that this world is reconciled to God by Jesus Christ and my responsibility now is to adequately, accurately communicate that great truth and let them know that they're free.*

And then, he closed his presentation with a beautiful prayer.

The atmosphere was thick with tension. It soon became obvious that his peers had formed their responses well before his presentation concluded, perhaps even before it even started. In response, individual bishops took the podium, each presenting to Bishop Pearson his own fifteen- to twenty-minute scriptural rebuttal, explaining why the Gospel of Inclusion was inaccurate and heretical. After the last panelist finished his rebuttal, there was a question-and-answer period. The panelists selected a total of four questions from the audience. At the end of the Q & A, Bishop Ellis took to the podium and thanked Bishop Pearson for coming, thanked the panelists for their responses, and the audience for their questions. He then said he wanted to give one final observation and one final announcement.

Bishop Ellis shared a story about a visit and a discussion he'd recently had with a Dr. Marvin McMickle, a professor at Ashland Theological Seminary. He began by speaking light-heartedly about a conversation they had about different religious practices. He then concluded two points from reading Bishop Pearson's material. His first conclusion was, "It is God's party and God can take into Heaven anybody He wants to because it's His." His second conclusion was that God had given only one plan for getting to Heaven, which was repentance and faith in Jesus Christ. With a tone of indignation, Bishop Ellis continued: "That's where I think traditional Christian doctrine stands, at least this afternoon. I'm still where I was when I got started."

Bishop Ellis's proclamation that traditional Christian doctrine was essentially stuck in one place was exactly right! That is where traditional Christian doctrine stands! And yes, he was right again when he said that he was still in the same place as he was when he got started. And perhaps that's the place he'll always be. It's not a good thing or a bad thing. It's not even something to judge. It's just how he sees things and interprets what God shows him. But Bishop Ellis was just one person; it was not his place to discredit what God had revealed to another individual. Just as Martin Luther and Bishop Mason each heard from God in his day, was it not possible for God to speak differently to people as they evolved to gain a deeper understanding of their call? It's crazy for me to think that any of us can know all there is to know about an infinite God. God is God!

Still holding the mic, Bishop Ellis continued with this:

> *There will be a written response to our brother and this College will answer the Commission. We'll prepare it and send it to the Board and we will then mail it to our contemporaries in this joint college. I told Bishop Pearson, when I first talked with him, that we reserve the right to respond in writing, and we also reserve the right to say whether or not we believe that what he espouses is heretical, and that we also reserve the right to say whether or not we*

believe what he is teaching and preaching is Christian
or absolutely false. And we love him with the love of
the Lord, but we will withdraw any fellowship from
him. We will not make any pathway for him to
evangelize any more than we would for Louis
Farrakhan.

And with mic in hand and a smile on his face that led to a
big-teeth grin, Bishop Ellis peered over his glasses and looked
down at the audience and said:

That's the position that the College takes so far! Let's
see what the Commission says. They may be even
nicer than I am. I'm sort of lurid and medieval; I still
believe in doom and damned with the devil and his
angels. Yes, I was scared of hell, the saints scared the
hell out of me. That's why I got saved, to keep from
going there. I believe it exists, I'm a little warm now.

Then he turned toward the board of Bishops and said,
"We're in the hands of the Dean of the College. While I escort
our guest out, would you stand? Just stand out of respect for
his exit." They did, and Bishop Pearson was ushered out of
the auditorium past the audience, in the same fashion as a
trespasser would have been escorted from the premises. It
was a public and humiliating denunciation, an ambush in the
truest sense of the word, one orchestrated by the Evangelical
Elite.[1]

When Bishop Pearson returned to Tulsa, he continued to preach his conviction. Although he mentioned that he had been formally declared a heretic, none of us at the church were fully aware of the severity of those proceedings. None of us knew exactly what was said and how he was treated. In the years since, of course, the recordings of that entire meeting have been posted online; as of this writing, they are available for anyone to view on YouTube. But Bishop Pearson himself never really let on, and he never lashed out. He was hurt by the broken fellowship with his peers, but he was fueled by his belief that everyone was, indeed, included in God's love.

Despite all the twists and turns of that year, Higher Dimensions held services each week with as much normalcy as possible. We celebrated each holiday as usual, although with far fewer people present than in previous years. More evidence of my healing was the fact that once-dormant interests were now beginning to reawaken in me.

As I explored my own thoughts and questions about God's all-inclusive love, I was given a unique opportunity. As a child coming of age in our little country church, I often participated in the various skits and plays that my mother directed. I must have inherited that gene from her. Now, I felt the need to do something for the church that expressed, in a creative way, what Bishop Pearson was preaching. My vision to write and produce a stage play came to fruition that year in our Christmas production, titled *A Taylor Made Christmas.*

The story centered around the places life can take you when you are led by your fears. In the play, the main character, Sedrick Taylor, loses his executive position and is afraid to tell his shopaholic wife that he is unemployed. Sedrick encounters various characters—the boisterous bartender, the promiscuous, femme fatale, "Sassy;" the gay "Juwann," and the alcoholic minister—all of whom help him to discover a new perspective on life. But it takes Sedrick reaching his lowest point to see them all as included in God's love. The play emphasizes how God can use anybody, anywhere, in any stage of life, to touch you in just the way you need.

Although our numbers had dwindled, all of the talent we needed to put on the production was right there in the church. The play was received well, and even attracted the curiosity of a few people from other churches. It didn't reverse our decline, however. Yet, it was a fun distraction that enabled us to have a new focus and spend quality time with each other as the Christmas holidays approached. It also made me see that my mother was still alive in me in more ways than I realized. *A Taylor Made Christmas* was revamped and repeated the following year.

I never thought anyone was obligated to believe, understand, or agree with Bishop Pearson. I also never thought he would be so poorly treated because of his convictions. For months, I held back while I listened to the comments, the criticisms, and the accusations coming from every direction. I'd read article after article of opinions and half-truths. I'd watched as Christian people and leaders slowly turned their backs and detached themselves from us as if we had a contagious plague. By this time, my patience was beginning to wear thin.

I never knew it was possible to get "booted out" of the Christian world. But because Bishop Pearson wouldn't shut up and refrain from teaching the Gospel of Inclusion, they kicked him to the curb. For thinking outside the box, he was no longer welcome in their 'for-members only' Christian club. His intentions were irrelevant, and because the College of African-American Pentecostal Bishops did not accept his viewpoint, they unanimously agreed to mark him off their list. They rejected him—not because he committed murder, or rape, or adultery, or embezzlement, or any big crimes or sins—but because he was causing people to think that they were okay with God just as they were. Evidently, this was just as much of a sin as any. They publicly despised and rejected our leader without ever considering how their bitter, hateful, nasty spirits would affect us or his children and family. To me, their treatment of Bishop Pearson was about the most un-Christ-like thing I could ever imagine.

I didn't understand how the Christian world couldn't see the Gospel of Inclusion as a good thing. I thought it was what the Church taught all along. I really believed that God could do anything! Anything! That included erasing the need for a literal hell. I never put a cap on God's potential. I thought everyone kept evolving until they died and in the interim we were free to live and discover whatever we needed to discover, to believe whatever we truly believe. I thought that's what salvation was all about. To accept this version of God was never a question for me because I'd never locked God into any particular, permanent compartment. Furthermore, I was never sold on hell or the devil in the first place because neither held significance in my home when I was growing up. No one ever said they didn't exist, they just weren't emphasized. I just don't remember conversations about the devil or hell in my home.

When Bishop Pearson declared that everyone was saved whether they knew it or not, I didn't have to wonder what that meant. I knew what I had just gone through before arriving at Higher Dimensions Church. All I did to break free of that darkness was to finally realize who I already was and fully comprehend that I was that from the beginning. If, indeed, Jesus was the atoning sacrifice, and if, indeed, you really believed the Atonement worked, then that was good enough for me. And after years of internal misery and grief, good was exactly how I felt and the threat of hell was not factored into the equation.

So, why wouldn't God-loving people want to share this good news with everyone? The message of Inclusion was reality for me in many ways because that's how things happened to me. I didn't know it at first, but later came to realize that I am everything I'll ever need to be because God created me from the beginning already complete. When I heard Bishop

Pearson teach these things, it freed my mind from the load I once carried. I was awakened to my own spirit. I could not un-believe what happened to me just because it didn't fit in someone else's doctrine. I didn't go to Higher D looking for a doctrine; I went looking for peace and I found it already inside of me.

As Bishop Pearson continued to attract negative press from the church world, many of his speaking engagements were cancelled. Gospel artists were reluctant to keep their scheduled appearances at his events. Anxious about protecting their own reputations and careers, they were afraid to be seen supporting Bishop Pearson in any way. This blew my mind and hurt my heart!

We were watching him being stabbed in the heart and falling to his death right before our eyes, and we could do nothing to stop it. Every time we gathered, Bishop Pearson would try to reassure us that he was alright. "I'm not concerned about me," he would say, "but I want you to be alright." He looked and sounded okay, but the energy in the room let us know he wasn't okay. It was painful knowing that he was hurting inside. It was even more painful to realize that he was most harshly rejected by the people who once claimed they loved him so. And it all started because he had a new thought about God, a thought in his own mind that he never tried to force anyone else to believe; a thought he simply shared with his congregation inside of his own church just like he had shared many other sermons and stories.

This all forced me to rethink my own perception of the church and what it means when we say we are "Christian." Does it mean that we can never change our opinions or beliefs? Does that mean we can never have an original thought outside of what's printed in the Bible?

As people left the church, they assumed everyone would eventually leave. So it wasn't unusual to run into people who would ask me if I was still there. Most often, I tried to avoid the conversation, and when I did answer, my standard response was usually, "I'm still at Higher D because I have no reason to leave." To some, that may have seemed a little abrupt. But rarely did I feel the need to explain myself.

I was amazed at how bold the comments and criticisms were becoming. It felt like open season on Bishop Pearson and our church, and people had no reservations about speaking their minds, sometimes in the unlikeliest of places. I can remember standing in line to pick up my clothes from the cleaners when a loud-talking lady standing in line behind me asked if I used to sing in the Higher Dimensions Choir. I told her, "Yes, I'm still an active member of the choir." Before I could finish my sentence, she interrupted me and said, "Well, I'm surprised there's anyone left in the church at all. I used to love Carlton Pearson. My daughter and I used to go to his church every Sunday until he started preaching about the devil not being real. I think he's losing his mind, so we decided to find another church because my Bible clearly tells me there is a devil and a hell!"

I was stunned, but she continued: "I also heard he was getting a divorce. I bet Gina felt she had to get out of there too." This boisterous woman said all of this in one breath inside of a public place, knowing that others were listening to our conversation. Yet, she did so without regard for who I was or how I'd feel about her comments. As I paid for my clothes and turned to walk toward the door, I turned and smiled at her and said, "I'm afraid you got it wrong on all counts, and it'd serve you best if you knew your facts before you start talking next time." Then I gave her that most famous of Christian lines in my most sarcastic tone: "You have a blessed day, now!"

Hearing derogatory comments had quickly become the norm for those of us who remained at Higher Dimensions. Seemingly, every week there was something or someone else condemning us. In a moment's notice, we had to decide whether to defend ourselves, defend him, defend our church, or just walk away in silence.

But there were a few who were genuinely concerned. Some of our family members needed reassurance that we weren't members of some strange cult. Even a few years after the initial "shock" of the Inclusion message had worn off, the people who loved us most couldn't understand why we hadn't come to our senses. They felt compelled to reach out.

On November 10, 2007, I received the following email from my sister living in the Los Angeles area:

Hi Sis, I want to tell you something that's been on my heart for a long time, but I didn't know how to say it. Please don't take offense before reading the whole thing and praying about this, because I believe I am in God's timing for this E-mail. Here are some scriptures I want you to read concerning your Leader's teaching:

2 John 1:8-11 (the Living Bible): "Beware of being like them, and losing the prize that you and I have been working so hard to get. See to it that you win your full reward from the Lord. For if you wander beyond the teaching of Christ, you will leave God behind; while if you are loyal to Christ's teaching, you will have God too. Then you will have both the Father and the Son. If anyone comes to teach you, and he doesn't believe what Christ taught, don't even invite him into your home. Don't encourage him in any way. If you do you will be a partner with him in his wickedness."

Gal 1:8 NIV. says "But even if we or an angel from heaven should preach a gospel other than the one we preach to you, let them be eternally condemned."

2 Peter 2:1-3 NIV talks about "false teachers among us" and how " they secretly introduce destructive heresies, even denying the sovereign Lord who bought them, bringing swift destruction on themselves. Many will follow their depraved ways and will bring the way of truth into disrepute. In their greed these teachers will exploit you with stories they have made up."

There are many other scriptures. These are just a few. 1 John 4:1, Acts 20:29-30, also Rev 22:18, Deuteronomy 4:2, and Proverbs 30:6 all warn us of adding to or taking away from the Bible. In Revelations, it says God will take away from him his share in the tree of life. Proverbs 30:5 says, "Every word of God is flawless."

I want you guys to know that I love you, and I am not trying to tell you what to do; only pray and make sure you hear from God.
Your Sis,
Carolyn

I received her words with no resistance. I considered and weighed what she said and used her message as a guideline to check myself. I could have been offended that she had carefully selected scriptures for me to read but I wasn't. This was my big sis, and I was obligated to stop, listen, think about what she had to say, and give her my most authentic response. She was genuinely concerned for my wellbeing and I appreciated her reaching out to me. Discerning the sensitivity of the issue, I needed to reassure her that I hadn't lost my mind, nor was I blind to what was really going on. This was my response:

> *I appreciate your concern, and I never take offense to anyone's advice or caring attitude when sharing out of love; but please trust that I know God for myself in accordance with my own experiences, studies, and struggles. Know that I am not under the influence of any man but have my own understanding of who God is, even before and apart from Bishop Pearson's leadership. There is no man on earth that can distract, or teach, or cause me to fall because of his belief. I know what I know because of my own connections. When Jesus asked, "Who do you say I am?" that, to me, means who do I believe he is in accordance with MY understanding and life's experiences. I know that all don't agree and all don't have to. But where I live in my heart, and what I know about God for myself and not through Bishop Pearson or anyone else for that matter, has to be what's right for me.*
>
> *Things may not look the same, or sound the same, but where I am is where I need to be. That came straight from God for me and until He says otherwise I have to*

stay the course no matter what anybody else says. I've spent the last ten years of my life with so much alone time with God. I KNOW that I hear His voice. I KNOW that He speaks to me, and I KNOW when to move or stay put. I am aware that this is the road less traveled; nevertheless, it is the road I must take. You just have to trust that God is big enough to bring me through it. I have many choices in churches and leaders here in Tulsa, as there is a church on every corner. BUT God says to stay put and that I must do until He says different. Where I am walking now may not be for everyone to walk or even to understand, or agree with, but it is in direct line with my purpose and His instructions, so that I will do. No one knows what my life has been like or the things that I've gone through. I only know this: I am certain of my understanding of who God is in my life, and that He, indeed, orders my steps. I won't detour for anyone's sake but His. I love my Bishop, but he is a man like every other leader. What I am doing is following the voice of God as He has revealed Himself to me.

I do thank you for reaching out. That is the one thing that I always wondered about with the rest of the religious world. If they were at all that concerned, I would think they would have come for us instead of just ridiculing and damning us all to hell. But just know

that it is God that I am following and I am clear on what
He is saying to me. I appreciate your emailed scriptures
and concern, but just trust that God knows what He is
doing with me as crazy as I am.

With Love,
Your Sis

This was our sole conversation about the issue. We never spoke of it again. I still don't know what part she agrees with or disagrees with fully, but it all seems so irrelevant now. Because we love each other as a family, there has been no division between us because of Inclusion. I believe that choosing to consciously allow love to override differences in any situation is what pleases God most! How my sister and I handled the situation is what I expected from the church.

CHAPTER 11

"We still had a mortgage and utilities to pay..."

-Teresa

Pastor Carlton's shift in doctrine was becoming more than just a local or regional news item; increasingly, it was becoming a topic of national interest. Even before his denunciation by the Pentecostal College of Bishops, the Gospel of Inclusion was attracting the attention of Christian media. With more than a quarter of a million readers, *Charisma Magazine* was (and, as of this writing, continues to be) one of the most important Evangelical news outlets in the country. By April 2002, *Charisma* published an article titled "Pearson's Gospel of Inclusion Stirs Controversy." In it, writer Eric Tiansay immediately underscored the contrast between accepted Protestant theology and Pastor Carlton's "controversial view":

> The *Tulsa Beacon* reported that Pearson has been confronted over his teaching by televangelists John

Hagee, Marilyn Hickey and his mentor, Oral Roberts. Roberts, Hagee and Hickey declined to comment about the matter.

Continuing, Tiansay pointed out that TD Jakes, however, was not silent:

> Jakes . . . told *Charisma* that he repudiates Pearson's views as heresy. "While I do consider Carlton Pearson to be a friend, I believe his theology is wrong, false, misleading and an incorrect interpretation of the Bible," Jakes said in a statement. "Carlton...improperly characterizes me as not being 'bothered' by this. I am both bothered and troubled by this teaching and with any implication that I support or in any way agree with it."[1]

This *Charisma* article was followed by a series of other articles, each a tabloid-like critique of Pastor Carlton's deceptive doctrine and fall from grace. Later that same year (September 2002), *Charisma* published another article, "Controversy Clouds Pearson's Ministry," reporting, almost gleefully, it seemed, that "People are leaving the Oklahoma pastor's church because of questions about his doctrines."[2]

Fortunately, we got more than just negative coverage. Investigative reporters from the secular media began to take notice. At first, Pastor Carlton's shift in theology seemed to be a pretty church-specific item of interest. But when the nightly news came calling, it was clear that Pastor Carlton had touched a nerve, not just with devout Christians but with millions of people who had questions about their own eternal fate.

Tulsa has always been a hub for orthodox Evangelical thought. This is a city known for its sheer number of churches per square mile, not to mention its many megachurches that dwarf the smaller ones. The Azusa Conference was just one of several religious conferences known for attracting thousands to Tulsa each year. So when local journalists did their investigations into Pastor Carlton's departure from orthodoxy, they found no shortage of local ministers willing to comment.

In September 2002, journalist Terry Hood, of Tulsa's *News On 6*, did a report on Pastor Carlton. As a responsible investigator, she maintained her own objectivity, offering viewers both sides of the story. She invited Pastor Carlton to give his argument but also invited megachurch pastor Billy Joe Daugherty of the gargantuan Victory Christian Center to comment. Of course, he disagreed with the Gospel of Inclusion, citing what he called its "danger." Daugherty said, "[If] We say everyone's saved, then we stop multitudes of people from coming to Christ." To Terry Hood's credit, however, she remained detached and above the fray, offering her report in a way that at least allowed viewers to wonder.

Unwittingly, perhaps, Daugherty pinpointed the real

concern: the multitudes. I will never believe that these pastors were actually concerned about individual souls. Instead, they were worried about the multitudes, the crowds of people, working people who faithfully brought tithes and offerings to pay for exorbitant, ostensibly "religious" operations and flamboyant lifestyles.

In 2002, websites and social media also started to unleash a flood of Christian hatred so putrid that it was difficult to tell whether the disdain was for Pastor Carlton's "Gospel of Inclusion" or for Pastor Carlton himself. The venom spewed at Pastor Carlton was often wrapped in a veneer of Christian concern for his spiritual wellbeing. Most often, however, his "fallen" status seemed to beacon opportunists far and wide, other preachers eager to use the occasion for their own self-aggrandizing moment in the spotlight.

In June of 2004, *Charisma* published an article that added more fuel to an ever-growing fire. The article reported on the proceedings of the African-American Pentecostal Bishops, during which Bishop Carlton Pearson had been officially denounced as a heretic. The article also mentioned a seventeen-page paper written by the group's doctrinal commission chairman stating that the College would no longer offer to Bishop Pearson its hand of fellowship. Furthermore, they strongly urged all their fellow members to refuse Bishop Pearson access to their pulpits. The *Charisma* article gathered commentary from other Evangelical ministers who expressed their concern about Bishop Pearson's apostasy.

Among others, it cited Ted Haggard, president of the National Association of Evangelicals, which represented some forty-five thousand congregations and millions of followers nationwide. Haggard described Bishop Pearson's teaching as "inaccurate and counterproductive to the cause of Christ." [3]

In a later *Charisma* article, the writer was much more damning. In 2005, J. Lee Grady's "We Need Tough Love," declared:

> Paul believed that when heresy goes unchecked it contaminates everyone. He warned his disciple Timothy that false teaching spreads "like gangrene" (2 Tim. 2:17). "Gangrene" can also be translated cancer. Modern translation: False doctrine is malignant. Get the tumor out before it kills people. It troubles me that many charismatic and Pentecostal church leaders today are not displaying the necessary backbone to label a heretic a heretic. We have become masters at soft-pedaling and inaction when the Lord requires us to confront. Case in point: Bishop Carlton Pearson, who was raised in the nation's largest Pentecostal denomination (the Church of God in Christ) and who once worked with the Oral Roberts Evangelistic Association, began teaching what he calls "the gospel of inclusion" a few years ago. He has become a Universalist, claiming that people do not need

conversion in order to be saved by Christ. Pearson's deception has been widely reported. In *Charisma* we followed Pearson's demise and announced that one organization, the Joint College of African-American Pentecostal Bishops' Congress, labeled him a heretic . . . . Since then Pearson has convened a national conference about Universalism that featured John Shelby Spong, an Episcopalian who affirms gay ordination and does not believe in the resurrection of Jesus Christ. You would think that every charismatic leader in the United States would sever ties to Pearson until he renounces his apostasy.[4]

With his shift in doctrine, Pastor Carlton opened the floodgates, unleashing for money-hungry pastors around the city a multitude of Higher D defectors now in search of new church homes, churches eager to accept a fresh infusion of tithes and offerings. At least a half dozen of the former Higher D ministerial staff started their own churches or evangelical ministries, each taking a few former Higher D members with them. Some were rather bold in their recruitment tactics.

I remember going out to my car at the end of one Wednesday evening service to find that a colorful, neon flier had been tucked beneath one of my windshield wipers. I glanced at the other cars in the parking lot to see the same flier. The flier was placed there by the pastor of a new church, a former Higher D minister who had left in protest. He'd started his own church, and the flier was a brazen invitation for us to abandon the flailing Higher D and attend his services instead. In the corporate world, such a practice would be considered illegal. Boldly recruiting on the grounds of your competitor is both unprofessional and highly unethical. In the church world, however, this disregard, for both feelings and boundaries, had become commonplace.

While the Christian media had its field day with us, we continued to meet for services, returning each time to find that the congregation had become yet fewer in number. James and I were lay elders by this time and were invited to meetings about the state of the church's financial affairs. By 2004, the membership had fallen so much that entire rows of unnecessary seats were removed from the sanctuary. When the remaining congregants occupied fewer seats, the crowd appeared to be less anemic. But the sudden appearance of large areas of bare floor was lost on no one.

The members who left Higher D took their money with them. Although the offerings were greatly diminished, the expenses remained. We had been left with a huge debt from the last, failed Azusa Conference. The church had fronted the money for thousands of out-of-towners who never showed up to occupy the blocks of hotel rooms that were reserved. We still had a mortgage and utilities to pay, grounds to maintain, staff to support. Higher D always had a reputation for compensating its staff handsomely. Ironically, the church was relieved of paying the highest salaries when most of the pastoral staff resigned in protest to Pastor Carlton's teaching.

All of the white pastoral staff left at once. Despite whatever they might have claimed, the racial overtones of this gesture were difficult to ignore. As a black woman, from an exclusively African-American religious background, the multiracial blend of Higher D was always a source of fascination and pride to me. Before Higher D, my close and regular interaction with people beyond my race was confined to school and work. In those contexts, however, my guard was always up. I could never afford to be vulnerable or completely transparent. I was always required to be on my A-game, both to prove my worthiness to be there, and to confront any hostility with dignity. I had several white coworkers and friends who I considered dear and close; however, for African Americans, a certain self-preserving posture is just a fact of life.

Church was in a different category. At Higher D, I could let down the guard and open myself to the spirit of God, with praise, joy, pain, tears, and all. It was the one place that I could be with large numbers of white people and not feel the need to protect myself, or to present myself as though coming up for inspection. At Higher D, the Holy Spirit was the great equalizer, not erasing our racial differences, but reconciling them in a way that made our fellowship with each other more important than our backgrounds. To be fully black and fully connected to non-blacks in the spirit, that was a beautiful thing. So when the white pastoral staff all left together, it made me question whether the connection I felt was as authentic as I wished for it to be. Had I just imagined that there was racial openness and equality at our church? Or did the white staff leave because they felt that Pastor Carlton was now utterly beyond their control?

1. Tiansay, Eric. "Pearson's Gospel of Inclusion Stirs Controversy." *Charisma Magazine*, 30 April 2002.
2. Gillespie, Natalie Nichols. "Controversy Clouds Pearson's Ministry." *Charisma Magazine*, 30 Sept. 2002.
3. Gaines, Adrienne S. "Black Pentecostal Group Denounces Carlton Pearson as Heretic." *Charisma Magazine*, 30 June 2002.
4. Grady, J. Lee. "We Need Tough Love." *Charisma Magazine*, 30 Nov. 2005.

CHAPTER 12

"But he was my friend. But he was gay."

– Teresa

The church was hemorrhaging members. By 2004, what had been a megachurch of thousands had shrunk to a remnant of a few hundred who continued to lean in and listen carefully to Pastor Carlton's teaching. This idea that Christ had purchased free salvation for all—even my unrepentant father—was something that never got old for me. Each time I went to church, as sparse as the crowd had become, I couldn't wait to hear it again. The more I listened, the more I researched on my own; the more I did my own research, the more Pastor Carlton's teachings were confirmed in my own thinking. Digging deeply into my fossilized religious assumptions generated more questions, none of which were too unsettling for God to handle. I raised these questions with God in my own prayer time, never once feeling that I had veered off into some forbidden territory. I was particularly bothered by the fact that so many of us

Christians were completely okay with hell and with millions going there—in fact, insisting on it. I was still praying; God was still answering. I could still sense the Anointing of the Holy Spirit, both in the privacy of my own devotions and whenever we gathered. The Anointing was still there—quieter now, perhaps, because the crowds had dissipated. But there was a new intimacy we felt, the little core of us that remained, and a fresh authenticity in the way we interacted with each other.

The crowds now gone elsewhere, Higher D was no longer a megachurch. Along with the reduction in population, however, came a change in demographic. Pastor Carlton's message began to attract people that we had not seen before. Hindus in their tunics and saris, openly gay couples, and the clearly "unchurched" began to trickle in and attend our services, obviously hearing in Pastor Carlton's new message something that resonated with them. Although it was painful to let go of friendships that seemed now irreparably severed, it was also intriguing to begin to see, for the first time, how big and diverse the world—God's world—really was.

Among those who remained, there were those who were comfortable with the concept of Inclusion but uncomfortable with homosexuality. My Pentecostal upbringing made quite clear—from the pulpit, at least—that homosexuality was an abomination, a sin, something to be forgiven and corrected, but never, ever normalized or accepted. As a youngster, however, I easily recognized the gay men among us at Open

Door Refuge Church of God in Christ. They were deacons, ushers, and choir members, some trying desperately to feign heterosexuality, even to the point of marrying and having children.

Two young men, both of whom stood as groomsmen in my older sister's wedding at my childhood church in the early 1980s, were gay. I was just a teenager back then, quite sheltered and avowedly naive about the world. Yet, I could see and sense their angst, their faithful return, time and again, to the one place where they felt both God's acceptance and His church's rejection. They kept their heads down, were humble, friendly, and compliant. They sang, shouted, and praised, went to Sunday School, and put their coins in the offering plate just like the rest of us. They heard all the same sermons I heard, the whole catalog of sins to dread, to avoid, and to confess. They heard our fiery preacher use hateful terms like "faggot," "sissy," and "bulldagger" in the name of God. In my Pentecostal upbringing, there was no space for anyone to say, "But I was born this way." God didn't make mistakes. These two young men each died alone in their thirties from what we now know was, very likely, AIDS.

In high school, I was immersed in music and participated in the marching band, the jazz band, the concert band, in orchestra, and in programs and musicals of all kinds. These were the early days of my lifelong involvement in the arts, music, in particular. The arts have always been a community for creative misfits. As an odd-looking "sanctified" girl, I was a misfit in my own way. Several of my very good musician friends who also played in band and orchestra were misfits too, some of them mocked and teased for being different. Although he never spoke of it, one of my closest friends was clearly gay. But he was my friend. But he was gay. But he was my friend—an internal tug-of-war for me, an irritating cognitive dissonance with no resolution.

I went through high school and college aware of gay people, friends with a few of them, but sad for them in general. I mentally assented to the assumption that they were choosing this abomination and could change if they just surrendered their lives and prayed hard enough. Yet, it didn't seem fair that they had this special burden and I didn't.

My pursuit of a Ph.D. did nothing to dissuade me from the teachings of childhood. In 1991, however, my friend Crystal, a fellow doctoral student at Indiana University, laid bare my hypocrisy. We were on a long bus ride headed, with other scholars from Bloomington, to an academic conference in Iowa. In the seat in front of us was a young woman with a Bohemian appearance, thick dreadlocks, dark, military-style clothing, and a quiet, reclusive demeanor. There was a masculinity about her that made me uncomfortable enough to reach inward in search of my moral superiority. Crystal, however, having no religious baggage, accepted her immediately. In her own gregarious, open, and transparent way, Crystal began to make conversation with this woman, asking her name, her field of study, where she was from, etc.

Crystal befriended her and invited her to talk openly and comfortably about who she was, where she'd met her partner, how long they'd been together. In the space of that bus ride, Crystal humanized and embraced her in a way that my religion forbade me to. Near the end of the trip, Crystal pulled me aside and confronted me: "And so you really think she's going to hell, right?" I responded the only way that I knew to at the time: "That's what the Bible says." My response was rote, hollow, and sterile. And it felt wrong. All wrong. But it was the only script I had.

As members of the LGBTQ community began to frequent Higher Dimensions, their presence was the deal-breaker for some. There were those who could accept inclusion, but sitting beside a same-gender-loving couple was where they drew the line. And so our numbers grew even smaller.

CHAPTER 13

"We barely broke even, and time was running out."

-Teresa

The year 2005 was the longest in the history of time for us, one that seemed to drag on for eons. The handwriting was on the wall. Our church was in dire financial straits, and we continued to try and desperately hold on to property that was too large and too expensive for our small contingent of outcasts to maintain. At each service, we had begun the practice of collecting not one but two, and sometimes three offerings. Each time we gathered for worship, there was this nagging awareness in the back of our minds that the week's budget was more than likely not met, and we were sinking deeper and deeper into a hopeless pit of debt. We had all seen the graphs at the leadership meetings, showing the steady rise in our expenses and the steady decline in our revenue. We all felt the pinch. James and I were giving thousands of extra dollars to the ministry by this point, as were others. And yet, our thousands were but a drop in the bucket of the church's overwhelming needs. Previously, a single appeal in one of the well-populated worship services was sufficient to erase a five-figure need. Now, with just a few hundred of us left—most of us giving to the utmost extent of our ability—five-figure offerings seemed for us further and further beyond the realm of possibility.

We were already outcasts, so Pastor Carlton had nothing to lose by inviting Bishop Yvette Flunder to come and speak at our church. We were thrilled to welcome her and excited that she would sing with what was left of our choir by that point. Like Pastor Carlton, Bishop Flunder had deep roots in Pentecostalism and had been born and raised in the Church of God in Christ. It was the sanctified church and its culture that flavored her familiar style of preaching and singing. But she was a lesbian. Bishop Flunder was openly involved in a relationship with a woman for more years than most of us had been married. A sort of Mother Theresa, Bishop Flunder's ministry in San Francisco was to the lowest of the low, same-gender-loving people who were social outcasts, some of them homeless, infected with and dying of AIDS.

The only way to truly identify with the despised, the downtrodden, and the rejected, is to become one of them. We were beginning to understand. With our church all but abandoned and falling into obvious disrepair, many of our friends gone, our pastor labeled a False Prophet, and our financial resources dwindling away, we were beginning to get it. And there was Yvette Flunder, herself an expert in life on the fringe, taking out time from her flock in California to come to Tulsa and minister to us. Along with our now fifteen-voice choir, she sang the lead in a gospel oldie by Walter Hawkins called "Special Gift." The song speaks of being freed from prison, darkness, and the storms of life through God's grace. In our broken, yet hopeful state, we heard new meaning in those lyrics. Now, those words were personal for us. With Bishop Flunder on lead, we sang them, the few of us, with fresh inspiration.

At the end of that service, I needed to do what I'd never been able to do before that moment. I needed to repent—honestly, openly, full-on—for my hypocrisy, for my self-righteousness, for my judgmental assumptions. I needed to purge myself completely of the residue that kept me separate from any other child of God. I needed to find Bishop Flunder and come face to face with her, and rather than look away or create my own narrative of her existence, I needed to look her square in the eyes. After the close of that service, there was a short line of well-wishers visiting with her, thanking her for her message. When they had gone, I made my way to her, reached out and embraced her in tearful shame and humility. She didn't know my sin, but she forgave me, nonetheless, embracing me right back, healing me that night of my ignorance and my arrogance.

Our ever-shrinking congregation did everything in its power to put a positive spin on our dismal situation. With the best of intentions, a few of the choir members organized an appreciation service for Pastor David. He had served faithfully as Minister of Music for several years by that time, and it was common knowledge by this point that neither he nor the rest of the staff were getting regular paychecks. A genius and a master musician, David Smith was well-known and highly regarded by gospel artists around the country. He was the mainstay on many of our recording projects, and it seemed strange even to me that Pastor David remained at Higher Dimensions even as other, lucrative opportunities certainly beaconed him elsewhere. After most of his other colleagues on the ministerial staff had departed, he was solid, stable, fully committed to our dying church. Along with Pastor Jesse Williams, David remained faithfully supportive of Pastor Carlton.

The effort to honor Pastor David was sincere, but it backfired. Because Pastor David had known, played, and recorded with Gospel Music Royalty for decades, invitations were sent far and wide for people to come to Tulsa and join us in honoring him at a special service scheduled for 3:00 on that Sunday afternoon. It was a beautiful, sunny autumn afternoon, and we hoped that people could put aside their theological misgivings about our church long enough to honor someone whose contribution to the music ministry was unquestioned.

But the response was paltry. The crowd that turned out was anemic. The disappointment in the whole event was too thick for the energy and the enthusiasm we tried so hard to generate. Yelling "Can you give God some praaiiiise!!!" is very effective when the building is full and everyone is on the same theological page. But that same phrase to a crowd of one hundred and fifty in a room eighty-five percent empty has an entirely different impact. The remnants of our choir and the few remaining musicians felt duty-bound to give our best effort to the small audience of well-wishers who responded to the invitation and came to the service. But song after song, the smiles we wore to mask our disappointment in the outcome became increasingly plastic. The organizers of the event were devastated. Pastor David was publicly embarrassed and understandably so. It was a crushing blow and a waste of time.

Another effort to generate money was the establishment of a new, "Can Do" Ministry. The spirit of this effort was borrowed from the traditions of the Church of God in Christ, where people of limited means, for generations, successfully rallied to pull off various projects, like the purchase of property, the burning of mortgages, and the like. One of the successful entrepreneurs in the church, Fred Jackson, coordinated the Can-Do Ministry and organized the sale of dinners after Sunday services, just as the COGIC folks used to do in the old days. The dinners were delicious, and James and I became regulars. The crowd was now a fraction of what it had been, and these Sunday dinners afforded us opportunities to have actual conversations with people we may have never even seen back in the days when Higher D was thousands strong. Although we enjoyed getting to know people in a more intimate way, these dinners, despite the best of intentions, never really produced a profit. We barely broke even, and time was running out.

When things are clearly falling apart, we find some degree of temporary solace by showing the world our best impression of normalcy. Although our effort to pay the church's mortgage were stymied, we sought to boost morale in other, smaller ways. In black church tradition, the pastor's mode of transportation is considered to be a direct reflection on the congregation he serves. Said another way, a pastor driving a raggedy car is seen to have a flock that is obviously careless and irresponsible. Pastor Carlton needed a new car. This, however, seemed just another item on a long list of needs that were just as urgent. Again, with a big heart and the best of intentions, Fred Jackson rallied the congregation to pledge the monthly payments for the purchase of a new Mercedes. I thought that a Mercedes was ridiculous, given our financial desperation. This was no time for conspicuous consumption. Why not a good, solid Honda or Toyota? I kept my true thoughts to myself, however. In the spirit of supporting Pastor Carlton, who was being attacked from every side, James and I made our pledge to take on a month's payment. Still more money on top of the extra money we were already giving. Pastor Carlton got his car, and we paid our pledge. But some of those who pledged had hearts and intentions that were bigger than their wallets. With the multiple offerings, the futile attempts to fundraise, and efforts to smile through it all, church was becoming exhausting and tiresome, draining the few of us left for as much as it could squeeze. And yet, I believed in the message. I would not abandon Pastor Carlton, not now.

By 2005, our once pristine church building and surrounding acreage and property had begun to show signs of poor upkeep. The landscaping at the front of the church, once neatly manicured, was now attended to sporadically. There was a foul smell from the kitchen area, something similar to raw sewage, that greeted us at the South entrance. The Hammond B3 organ was out of commission, and there was no money to fix it, so Pastor David played the electronic keyboard instead. Our roof and entire heating and cooling systems were in need of maintenance that we could not afford. The beautiful water fountain that once graced the entrance to the church was silent and still, its rusting fixtures leaving brown stains on the pool's surface. The Christian celebrities, the gospel artists, and evangelical A-listers that once frequented our church no longer included Higher D on their circuit. It was during this time that James and I became more active and visible in our roles as lay elders, not because we were particularly gifted in any way, but because those who had previously occupied those positions were now gone. We had, as it were, become slightly bigger fish in an ever-shrinking pond.

In August of that year, the headline was Hurricane Katrina.

We were glued to our televisions as we watched coverage of New Orleans and the surrounding area. We were baffled at the colossal failure of the government to respond to the needs of the people there in jeopardy. The size and scope of the storm had been forecast and came as a surprise to no one; the thorough lack of preparedness was puzzling, to say the least.

The images of Katrina were haunting. We watched almost nonstop coverage of the thousands of hungry and tired who were huddled in the lawlessness and stench of the Superdome. We saw the reports of residents stranded on their rooftops unable to navigate their neighborhoods, which were entirely deluged with water. Our hearts broke at the sight of the bereaved who were unable to bury their dead—many of their lifeless, bloated bodies drifting aimlessly atop the filthy floodwaters. Katrina seemed a vivid depiction of the difference between poverty and privilege, between being saved and being lost.

As Katrina monopolized the national news, we were treading floodwaters of our own. At our church leadership meetings, there were more explanatory graphs on foreboding handouts, more dismal data, and we were becoming divided in our opinions about what should be done. I suggested that we sell the property while there was still enough equity to resolve our issues. I hated hearing myself say that; Higher D, after all, was home. We had important memories there, including our own wedding. But the inevitable reality was a bright warning light that had been flashing now for months.

The numbers did not lie.

The congregation and the money continued to shrink, the bills continued to pile up, and from week to week, the story wasn't changing. A storm—a big storm was on the horizon. It was just a matter of time before our property would be taken from us. Selling it, at least, allowed us to preserve our dignity and have some say in the matter. On the other side were those who insisted that we hang in there and fight—find a way to get the money that we needed. But how? What were we supposed to do? Rob a bank? Win the lottery? Call down dollar bills from Heaven? It boiled down to one simple fact: churches get their money from people. Unless there is a robust endowment, there must be people in the pews in order for the church to survive.

As we debated in these meetings, there sat Pastor Carlton, torn between the reality of the moment and his own ties to his life's work, ties that were a hundred times more powerful and personal for him than they were for any of us. He had birthed this entire thing, from the first service in Jenks, Oklahoma, to the development of the grounds on Memorial Drive, to the international draw of the Azusa Conference. For many years, a glass-encased, architectural model of Pastor Carlton's vision for the Higher Dimensions Ministry sat in the foyer just ahead of the entrance to the sanctuary. The miniature cardboard figures in the glass encasement depicted some future time when the ministry would consist of a beautiful compound of buildings on our grounds, at the center of which was our beloved sanctuary.

I was embarrassed by our situation. It ripped my heart out to imagine that the place I loved with every fiber of my being was slipping away. The air in that building was thick with so many memories—the powerful and electrifying praise and worship, our songs that shook the rafters, those we christened, baptized, and buried. My footprints and tear stains were in the carpet on the altar where I had often knelt to pray. I was embarrassed about our plight, and I was envious of those who enjoyed stability and normalcy.

After one Wednesday evening service, I drove by another church—a white church—which was about a quarter mile away from Higher D. On the marquee of that church, there was an announcement for a mortgage-burning celebration on the forthcoming Saturday night. These white people owned their property outright, free and clear. They could preach anything at all and never fear displacement. They could preach that Satan was love and still have the right to stay right there, even if their entire congregation scattered to the four winds. That is the power of ownership. When you are beholden to no one, there is nothing to fear. When you owe, you are stranded, uncertain, biding time on the top of a roof hoping for nothing but a miracle to make the filthy flood waters subside. You are helpless, watching the bloated bodies of your dead dreams drift here and there.

During that fateful year, news of our plight was generating intrigue in the secular media. The Christian media had made an Olympic sport of castigating Pastor Carlton and Higher D; the secular media, by contrast, was open and interested in the Gospel of Inclusion. We got a visit from National Public Radio and a producer there who found our story interesting. In the midst of our clear demise, we learned that NPR wanted to do a feature on Pastor Carlton for its popular radio show, *This American Life*. They found it unbelievable that a church could experience such a meteoric plummet just for preaching God's all-inclusive love. They came to Tulsa to do their own research and see for themselves, and they interviewed a few of us in the process. Their interest in us—minus the condemnation so typical of the religious world—was refreshing and encouraging. I was one of several they asked to interview. After sharing my experience and answering their questions, I never thought another thing about it. At the time, I was too heartbroken about our uncertain future to see this as the tiny light flickering at the end of the dark tunnel where we found ourselves.

As we approached the end of 2005, our mortgage troubles were well known in the local media. Then came the announcement we all dreaded: our last church service at Higher Dimensions on 8621 S. Memorial would be December 31st. The foreclosure settlement required that we vacate the property by January 1, 2006.

In its final weeks on life support, I inhaled as deeply as I could every time I entered the building, trying desperately to capture inside of my own body, for all of time, every memory that I could store. I knelt at the altar and ran my fingers through the plush, fuchsia carpeting on the pulpit, trying to imagine all of the tears that had fallen in that spot where people gave their lives to Christ, where babies were dedicated, and people got married, and healed and eulogized. I tried to imagine the sweat that had fallen from the brows of preachers delivering roof-raising sermons and singers giving their best. Knowing the end was near, some days after work I went there and I just sat and looked around, taking mental snapshots of every square foot that I could to store in the archival memory of my heart. Pastor David and the skeletal staff that remained were beginning to pack up their belongings. I took from the sanctuary one of the chairs, a chair that I purchased as a part of one of many failed fundraising efforts during the previous two years.

When the end finally came, James and I were out of town, visiting family in Louisville for the Christmas holidays. Although we were hundreds of miles away from Tulsa, we were every bit in mourning about the inevitable. The final Sunday service in our own sanctuary was Christmas Day, 2005. This awareness cast a shadow over our holiday spirit even as we celebrated with family members we hadn't seen all year. None of them knew what we were thinking or feeling; they only knew that we had been deceived into believing false doctrine, and they prayed that we would get saved again. Even though I knew my family loved me, and even though I completely understood their perspective, my mother's words were piercing: "I'm sorry about you all losing your church," she said, "but I don't agree with what your Pastor is preaching."

Perhaps that was something she needed to say, although it was nothing we needed to hear. The pain was enough without her commentary. And although her statement was a dagger through my heart, I knew that my mother would never, in a million years, say or do anything to intentionally hurt anyone, least of all one of her children. She is the most loving and Christlike person on the planet. It would literally destroy her to learn how her statement injured me that day. And for that reason, she will never know.

We detached ourselves from the Christmas festivities. We borrowed my sister's computer and went to her basement to watch the live streaming of the final Sunday service. We held each other and sobbed. The holiday party upstairs went on without us.

CHAPTER 14

"It was Christmas Day, 2005."

– Cassandra

Through a combination of classes, some held on the church grounds on weekends and others held online, I was able to complete my course of study at the Azusa School of Ministry. As I continued in my own personal growth and development, however, the church was in a steady state of decline. The cloud that hovered over the Higher Dimensions Church family during that season seemed to linger no matter what direction we took. Our weekly Sunday and Wednesday services continued as usual, always with hope that a miracle would come and turn things around financially. I never understood everything that was discussed in regard to what we needed to stay afloat, but I knew that the ministry could not survive as we were without a major financial breakthrough. Along with many meaningful and once-popular programs and opportunities that Higher Dimensions offered, the Azusa School of Ministry also faced its demise. Barely begun, by 2005, it, too, was discontinued, a casualty of our inability to generate income.

It was Christmas Day, 2005. I got up that morning, torn between the festive spirit of the holiday and the Sunday service for which I needed to prepare. My children and grandson were always part of my Christmas-day celebration, and we did the usual big breakfast and gift exchange. My six-year-old grandson, Terrance, had all of the normal excitement of a kid his age, and few things could bring me as much joy as watching him unwrap the gifts under the tree, most of which were for him.

With breakfast served and gifts exchanged, my thoughts and breaking heart turned to the part of the day that I didn't want to face. I dressed, combed my hair, put on my makeup, grabbed my purse and car keys, and headed out the door. I pulled out onto Memorial Drive, passing 31st Street, 41st Street, and continuing south, passing Christmas lights along the way. As I continued in the direction of the church, I kept thinking to myself that this was very much like that last drive from the funeral to the cemetery, that last trip that would afford me the opportunity to take one final glance at the place that I loved. It was because of the ministry at 8621 S. Memorial that I became alive again. Sitting in the back, in the corner, by a pole, unable to do much more than inhale, exhale, and exist, I heard words of life that restored me after the most devastating of losses. And now, that place that had given me life would be a loss of a different kind. At the same time that I felt pulled in the direction of the church, passing yet more Christmas lights, more festive scenes, my heart pulled away from this inevitable thing that was about to happen.

I entered the church and the choir stand, feeling a sense of uncomfortable finality. From where I sat, a haze seemed to settle over the sanctuary, a sort of fog thick in the atmosphere. I saw people, sullen in their expressions, still and frozen where clapping hands and shouting feet once had been. No one was smiling. There was nothing in that service that suggested that it was Christmas day.

Nearly a week later, on New Year's Eve, the dreaded end finally came. The proceedings of that final service were a blur. I don't remember what was said, except that Bishop Pearson was fragile that day. As much as he tried, it was clear that it was taking a toll on him. He had done all that he could to prepare us for it, but none of us really thought that our last day at 8621 S. Memorial Drive in Tulsa, Oklahoma would really come. I remember doing all I could to keep the tears from falling. I redirected my thoughts, closed my eyes, sang a little louder, smiled bigger and avoided direct eye contact with anybody else. I knew that once the tears started to flow, they would be impossible to stop. It all felt like a bad dream. I needed to wake up and handle my emotions. It was from the choir loft on the platform, standing behind Bishop Pearson, that I heard him give his last words in the Higher Dimensions building.

He had paused to gather his family near. Encircled in the

embrace of Gina, Julian, and Majeste', Bishop Pearson gave the eulogy of our life in that place. The court had ordered our congregation to vacate the premises. At the stroke of midnight, the building and the acreage on which it sat would no longer be ours. I had been fighting tears all day. But as I watched his family's tears begin to flow, my own tears, the ones that I had worked so hard to stall, began to stream down my face. Everyone in the sanctuary was crying, sharing in a general sense of bereavement and loss. And just like that, this chapter was over.

How do you suddenly let go of your entire church family, your place of growth, your place of healing, your place of learning, socializing, and support, not knowing what's next?

CHAPTER 15

"The feature, titled 'Heretic,' aired on December 16, 2005 …"

– Teresa

Although the Evangelical establishment in Tulsa squarely and unequivocally rejected Pastor Carlton, there were others in the city who reached out to us in ways that we didn't expect. In an incredible show of love and hospitality, Trinity Episcopal Church offered our tiny, homeless congregation the use of its sanctuary. Beginning on January 1, 2006, we met there on Sunday afternoons after Trinity's regular worship was done.

Trinity Episcopal was as different from Higher Dimensions as one could possibly imagine. In the heart of downtown Tulsa, their church was a stone cathedral with intricate stained-glass windows, elaborate wood altar carvings, varnished pews, and majestic, high ceilings. Their worship was scripted and liturgical. Their music, which echoed in waves due to the high ceilings and solid stone floors, was drawn entirely from the classical European tradition. Because it was situated in the heart of downtown Tulsa, Trinity Episcopal Church drew hundreds of homeless people every day to its feeding ministry, which was known as "Iron Gate," nicknamed for the place on the church grounds where the hungry gathered daily to wait in line for their meals.

For my lifetime of hearing about helping the poor, this was my first time as a Christian of ever going to where the poor were. This was my first time sharing actual worship space with this part of humanity, loved and included by God. They dressed in no finery and their worn backpacks and paper bags contained all they owned in the world. They had no tithes or offerings to give. These were the souls that many religious people preferred to ignore.

We wanted to become a part of the life of Trinity, so some months later, James and I volunteered for Iron Gate. While James was there serving breakfast, a man in the line struck him as familiar despite his dirty and tattered clothes and matted hair. The recognition was mutual. It turned out that the homeless man was a childhood friend of his. This man had grown up in his neighborhood, had done well in school, gone off to college, and had enjoyed a successful profession for a time. And then life happened; there he was, homeless, brought to nothing, and standing in line at a soup kitchen. That day, James offered his friend both a meal and words of encouragement and hope. Higher D had a feeding ministry, the Raven's Nest, for as far back as we could remember. But it dawned on us that such an experience at Higher D would have been highly unlikely because although we fed the poor, they had to come to us. Being at Trinity afforded us the opportunity, instead, to go to them, to share love with people who barely had the clothes on their backs, much less transportation to make the trip to South Memorial Drive. Hurting people are God's children. For any one of us, anything, at any time, can change.

As we began having our services at Trinity, we also resumed our regular schedule of choir rehearsals. While the sanctuary was stunningly beautiful, for our style of music, it was an acoustical nightmare. Our loud drums and hand-clapping, foot-stomping style of music was an exact mismatch for the resonance created by the high ceilings and stone floors. Due to the powerful echo, everything we sang sounded to us like this blurry wash of sound. The few remaining congregants complained that they could see us clapping and moving, but they couldn't understand a word we were singing, although we were singing from our hearts and through our grief with what we had left inside of our souls.

Although it was acoustically imperfect, we were grateful to have somewhere to go. Trinity's hospitality enabled us to remain connected to each other as a church body. We had no home of our own, but Trinity Episcopal gave us a temporary place to at least exist as a diminished version of ourselves. Although we were guests in someone else's home, the business of being a church family continued, as our remaining membership experienced the usual passages of life. We had at least three of our funerals while at Trinity, and probably some weddings too. This period gave us relief from the constant financial pressure that we felt during our final months at Higher D. It allowed us time and space to breathe again.

As we acclimated to our new environment, I forgot all about the NPR feature that was done before we lost our property on South Memorial. The feature, titled "Heretic," aired on December 16, 2005; this was around the same time that we were facing eviction and wrapping our minds around the reality of losing our church. I was completely unaware of the impact of that feature until I was stopped in the faculty cafeteria one day by a colleague of mine: "Hey, Teresa, was that you I heard on NPR? Weren't you interviewed for a show about Carlton Pearson on *This American Life*?" Other colleagues heard it, and friends from around the country emailed to let me know they'd heard the broadcast, even before I had a chance to hear it myself.

By midyear of 2006, "Heretic" had gained such momentum that major news outlets were taking a serious interest in Carlton Pearson and his tiny band of homeless followers. It was while we were at Trinity in August of 2006 that NBC's *Dateline* did a feature on Pastor Carlton's doctrinal shift, this time inviting commentary from Evangelical VIP Ted Haggard. At the time, Ted Haggard was the President of the National Evangelical Association. Keith Morrison asked for

Haggard's take, at which point he emphatically denounced the Gospel of Inclusion, making known his opinion that Pastor Carlton was way off the mark. A bevy of other ministers chimed in, publicly rebuking Carlton Pearson, all the while keeping their eyes on their own offering plates, all too aware of how expensive the wrong utterance could be.

Hollywood began taking notice. After months of exclusively bad news, a buoyant Pastor Carlton announced to us that Lisa Bonet was coming to Tulsa to visit with us. Lisa Bonet? *Denise Huxtable from The Cosby Show was coming to Tulsa?* She had heard the NPR feature and was fascinated with our story. She thought it would make a great script for a movie, and she and some friends were coming to Tulsa to explore the idea.

They came to our service and it seemed the oddest thing imaginable that Denise Huxtable was coming to worship and fellowship with us, even when our own friends would not. After the service, she and her two traveling companions spent time with us in one of Trinity's fellowship spaces, having casual conversation about the NPR broadcast and this Gospel of Inclusion. She was pleasant, down-to-earth, and genuinely interested in what we had to say.

Lisa Bonet came and went, but her visit revived us. We were tired and spent, and had grown accustomed to people running away from us. Having anyone come toward us was a blessing, and someone of her caliber making the time to visit and spend quality time with us was absolutely therapeutic.

The thought of a movie was intriguing, but seemed far-fetched to me. We were only trying to survive.

The normal transitions of life continued, and Trinity was our place to dedicate new babies and to eulogize our dead. The most gripping of those was the death of Jennifer, a beautiful young woman in her early twenties with a lovely spirit and perpetual smile. Jennifer was diagnosed with a serious illness during the end of our time at 8621 S. Memorial. Jennifer was special to us, not just because she was a delightful person, but because her decline seemed to parallel the decline of our church. As her disease progressed, she moved more and more slowly, but attended services, nonetheless, for as long as she could. As the numbers in our congregation continually diminished, sometimes it was the sight of Jennifer making her way painstakingly to her seat that lifted my spirit. Sometimes she came wearing house slippers and carrying the pillow from home that she needed in order to sit comfortably through the services; her smile was ever there, despite her pain.

As we made the transition from Memorial Drive to Trinity, Jennifer's condition continued to deteriorate. Her mother, Jean, sang tenor in our choir, and the remnant of us that remained grew especially close during that period. After a hard-fought battle, we got the call; Jennifer was finally at peace. Several members of the choir met Jean at St. John's Hospital, where we were invited to go to Jennifer's room, where she remained, having just passed away minutes earlier.

There she was, there—yet, no longer there, skin cold to the touch, lips slightly parted in a faint smile, forever young and gone too soon. A few days later, Jennifer's funeral was held at Trinity. The songs we sang for her service were slow, and there were no clapping hands or beating drums. So the sound carried beautifully in that acoustic space that day, echoing into the expansive ceiling, bouncing gently off of the stained-glass windows and stone walls. Jennifer was eternally fashionable in green, purple, and blue, her hair freshly styled, her face tastefully made up with a hint of pink lip gloss. She looked better there in her coffin than she had in months, however, she was gone. The heart-breaking relief, the bitter-sweetness of Jennifer's passing brought heavy tears. We celebrated Jennifer's brief but meaningful life and sang songs about healing and hope. And we cried, not only for Jean's excruciating loss, but because we had to say farewell to her in a house that belonged to someone else.

Sometimes death reunites the most estranged of family members. This was our experience when we lost one of our most beloved singers, Byron Davis. A popular gospel recording artist, and a staple of the Higher D choir for many years, Byron's death seemed jarring and sudden even though it came at the end of a long illness. It was known that thousands would come to pay their respects, and there could be no fitting tribute without the music that Byron loved. His family arranged to have the service at Greenwood Christian Center.

Greenwood was founded and pastored by Gary McIntosh, a close friend of Pastor Carlton's and a former associate pastor at Higher Dimensions. Well before the split over Inclusion, and with Pastor Carlton's blessing, Gary had already established his church in North Tulsa. The church was faring well. With the start of Inclusion, however, many of the former Higher D members who fled ended up there. Many jokingly called Greenwood "Higher D 2.0" because so much of its membership was transplanted directly from Higher D. Byron's funeral at Greenwood was a watershed moment for us. It was the first time that thousands of Higher D defectors and the remnant of Carlton Pearson supporters would be reunited in the same sanctuary.

The floor plan of Greenwood Christian Center was strikingly similar to Higher Dimensions. The entrance opened to a foyer, which then led to the sanctuary. Instead of pews, there were rows of hundreds of detachable chairs – the exact same type of turquoise chair that was in the Higher D sanctuary throughout the 1990s. At the front of the sanctuary was an elevated chancel where the ministers, choir, and musicians were stationed. This familiar layout, along with so many familiar faces, definitely gave a certain sense of going back in time to South Memorial Drive. But layered atop of the weird sense of déjà vu and the grieving was this thick blanket of awkwardness.

We were gathered there to celebrate Byron's life and memory. But the sanctuary was filled with a whole different collection of unspoken hurts, unasked questions, and unresolved animosity. My focus on Byron was compromised by the stew of emotions I felt. It was humiliating to be in a sanctuary that belonged to them while we had no property of our own. And it was their departure in droves that left us with no way to pay the mortgage. I felt angry that we could come together for a funeral, but not to talk out our differences and agree to disagree.

Even as Byron's hours-long funeral progressed, the division in the congregation was palpable. The choir assembled for the funeral service included both former Higher D and New D members, and it was beautiful that we could join our voices together again. That much, at least, was like old times, and I think Byron would have been pleased. Elsewhere in the congregation, however, the efforts to avoid eye contact were obvious. Minister after minister approached the podium to speak and pay their respects to Byron. Although Pastor Carlton was the common denominator of our gathering that afternoon, it was as though he was there—seated in the front row—yet not there. When Pastor Carlton approached the podium to speak, the reception was cordial, even subdued; nothing like the rousing applause and shouting that his very presence would have triggered in the old days.

Before leaving the funeral, I managed to exchange a few hugs with former Higher D members, people that I genuinely missed and was glad to see. But it was clear that there would be no further interaction between us, at least not until the next funeral. Life at Greenwood went on as usual. We resumed our meetings at Trinity.

Our time at Trinity attracted the downtrodden, the disaffected, and the curious. The message of Inclusion drew openly gay couples and transgender people who had been looking for a safe place to worship God. For some of our remnant, however, this was where to draw the line. As the gay presence grew increasingly obvious among us, there were people who considered this their tipping point and final stop on their journey with the church formerly known as Higher D. They had survived the controversy, the loss of our property, and the transition to Trinity. But the gay thing was impossible to tolerate. So they left, and our numbers became smaller still.

CHAPTER 16

"All of the remarks came from church-going people..."

– Cassandra

By 2006, the church had a skeletal staff, with the remaining few sometimes forced to multitask. Pastor Jesse Williams was one of those people who now did several jobs. My attendance at the Azusa School of Ministry enabled me to connect to many people, one of whom was Pastor Jesse. Although everyone knew him as the choir director, it was through our mutual connection to the School that I came to know him on a more personal level.

I was one of the first in my circle to begin experimenting with social media. Back before the days of Facebook, MySpace was all the rage. I had a MySpace page before it caught on. Pastor Jesse was intrigued with my page, and we talked often about how the possibilities of social media could be harnessed for Bishop Pearson and his message. It was in this way that I began assisting Pastor Jesse with Bishop

Pearson's social media posts and emails that year.

Bishop Pearson's MySpace followers grew to well over seven thousand people in no time. In 2008, his Facebook account was created, as MySpace began to lose popularity. His followers from MySpace transferred over to Facebook, and his friend-base grew so fast that a second Facebook and Group page were created to accommodate the additional fifteen thousand people who waited to be connected with him. Eventually, we created accounts on all social media platforms. Today, Bishop Pearson regularly posts and answers questions as his time allows with the assistance of his social media team. In those days, however, the growth of his web presence—which was in direct inverse proportion to the decline of his church—seemed sudden and overwhelming.

It was while managing Bishop Pearson's social media sites that I read many cruel, untrue, distasteful, and sometimes obscene comments that people were willing to publicly write both about and to him. It was easy to identify the church folks whose comments were prompted by leaders who had denounced Bishop Pearson. A blogger for "Tent Makers" stated in its article on the Gospel of Inclusion:

> *"Most of those who have rejected the message have done so not because they have thoroughly studied the subject in the Bible and have come to a conclusion against it, but because of what their pastors and Sunday School teachers have said about it."*

Those with a lynch-mob mentality had been given permission to lash out at him, and they did so every chance they got on every platform possible. [1]

I read social media posts, emails, and blogs that were so vulgar at times that I took it upon myself to delete them, something that Bishop Pearson will only discover once he reads this book. I determined that this hate mail served no purpose. He was already handling enough through his personal emails, postal-mail, and phone calls. Nevertheless, it didn't stop the comments from being posted.

Following is a sample of the kinds of hateful remarks that were now posted in the "comments" section of one of Bishop Pearson's once-popular videos. (Please note that these are shown verbatim from their original sources; the comments have not been edited.)

> *Carlton Pearson is a homosexual (pervert) that is why he so easily perverts the scripture...preaching nothing but damnable lies with the earring in his ear like TD Jakes ... frauds!*

> *Carlton Pearson is another idiot spewing blasphemy!*

> *This man is setting people up for hell. He is working for Satan. I wonder what he got out the deal. Child no way I would be working that hard for Satan and he not give me everything I could ever want or imagine.*

Pearson is teaching lies and is a false prophet. He is full of evil. He also lies as many in Christian circles never mention hell or the devil...Total liar.

WOW....this man is CONFUSED! Your Grandparents ARE in Hell, unless they came back to the Lord, after their backsliding.

You are one more fool on the most high's judgement list Carlton Pearson! Repent for the kingdom of Heaven is at hand. Shalom!!

And there were more comments on various Christian websites and blogs, such as these (unedited):

I feel so sorry for this man, but what he is preaching is false doctrine. His grandparents backslid and died in that state? so there is no more hell now? hell is only on earth he now says?? This man was grieving and his so called revelation about hell came from the devil. Yes there is a hell, and God said unrepentant sinners will go there, God changeth not.

Just watched Carlton, doesn't even look like the same man from years ago. The anointing was gone, it was sad. Even in his new church, appeared he was working it up out of the flesh. Why let pride take you down,

repent Carlton and get back on track! It's not too late.
He said accepting his new revelation was like steering a
big ship - takes time but finally you can make the turn.
Oh no, that's a slippery slope.

If we are born-again Christians, we must answer by
what we believe, and that is the Holy Bible. It is
possible Carlton could have gotten a more suitable wife
in his own fellowship in his church while younger, but
there are no guarantees. She posed as a born-again
believer and as I said before, he met her at a Christian
Singles Conference. The Bible says there are "wolves in
sheep's clothing." I'm still praying that he repents!

Bishop Pearson, has been turned over to a Reprobate
Mind. I remember hearing Carlton Preach for many
years and when I heard he was teaching this new belief
I could not believe it...The thousands he has preach to
for many years and became saved under his Preaching.
I hope you will not listen to this rotten doctrine he is
now teaching. He is leading many down a road to a sad
ending. If there is any hope for Carlton only God
knows. Everyone Pray for Carlton and ask God to
somehow change his thinking before it is too late. We all
need prayer for sure but God will not accept this
teaching from him. Carlton has studied the Bible and is
highly knowledgeable of what the Bible says and has

been fooled by Satan and if he does not change his teaching, I am afraid a terrible tragedy will come his way. I sure hope not, but all I can say is everyone Please Pray for Carlton! [2]

It's hard to continually read and listen to this kind of commentary about someone you hold dear. When you hear blatant lies and when you know that the people giving the commentary have no real insight into the subject of their remarks, it is difficult to stomach. All of the remarks came from church-going people with a sideline view. Funny thing is, all this time, I thought we church folks had vowed to hold ourselves to a higher standard when handling our differences and disagreements. If something out of the ordinary like this happens, we would at least know to withhold our judgements, research the facts, and then respond responsibly. There are respectable ways to handle every situation. Bishop Pearson never conducted himself in a way that would warrant the disrespect that he received from those who claimed they once loved him. To say I was disappointed would be a huge understatement.

The hatred on social media came to life on television. The vitriol continued for many years after we lost our church property. A classic example was an episode of the *Lexi Show* from 2009, during which Pastor Carlton was invited to speak on the Gospel of Inclusion. His message had been out for more than seven years at that time. Still, the reaction of the church people in the studio audience was animated to an almost mob-like degree. Jamal Bryant, another preacher guest on the show, held forth with eloquent indignation, presenting a sermon-like counterargument to Pastor Carlton's position. In his rhetorical bag of tricks were all the familiar quips, quotes, and Evangelical spins on scripture that usually send the righteous into a frenzy of self-affirmation.

When it comes to church, black people are traditionally vocal and responsive. During this show, however, as Bryant pointed out all of the reasons and ways that Pastor Carlton was wrong, the crowd's reaction reached fever pitch. The more Bryant held forth, the more the studio audience exclaimed its approval with "Hallelujahs!" and boisterous "Amens!". And the more the studio-audience-turned-congregation vocalized its approval, the more Bryant dug in, assaulting Pastor Carlton's message with a non-stop barrage of scriptures, all familiar, all heard a thousand times before. It was a cyclical orgy of the preacher feeding off the congregation feeding off the preacher, all delightfully watching as Pastor Carlton sat silent and composed, taking fire from every direction.

At the end of the mini-revival, the host, Lexi, stepped in to invite a response from Pastor Carlton, who should have been badly bruised by this onslaught. His response, however, was calm and dignified and came from a place of quiet strength: "God called me forward," he said. "I will not go back."

1. As of this writing, the online article, "The Dangers of Carlton Pearson's "Doctrine of Inclusion" (Universalism) [sic] can be found at the following URL:

http://www.tentmaker.org/articles/pearsons_doctrine_of_inclusion.htm.
2. The references to Carlton Pearson on social media are too numerous to cite here; the website is typical of much of the discourse around the Gospel of Inclusion. .http://christianblogs.christianet.com/carltonpearson.htm

CHAPTER 17

"He was suffering from exhaustion, maybe."

– Teresa

Standing about five feet and one inch and weighing about one hundred thirty pounds soaking wet, Pastor Jesse Williams, Jr. was a bundle of Holy Ghost energy. Impeccably dressed on even his worst days, he greeted everyone with an arresting smile and burst into choir rehearsals like a little dynamo ready to work the singers to death in the most loving way. He was already a veteran of the gospel music scene, a singer and songwriter whose music was known and loved by thousands. For several years, he was front-and-center at our Azusa Conferences, directing the three-hundred-voice choir. His outstretched arms had a reach extending all the way from the pounding heart in his little frame to the rafters of the massive auditorium. What he lacked in physical stature, he more than made up for in pure presence. His oft-repeated mantra, which he delivered with a dazzling smile, was "It's all good, 'cause it's all God!"

With most of the ministerial staff gone, Pastor Carlton's primary remaining supports were Jesse and Minister of Music, Pastor David Smith. With Jesse leading our shrinking choir and David at the keyboard, at least our music didn't suffer much. Choir rehearsals became even more of a type of therapy, as Jesse's relentless excitement could turn to fervent, tearful, cathartic prayer on a dime. And we followed his lead —praying, crying, weeping, and praising, all the while inexplicably grateful that we had each other.

A single man in his early forties, Jesse gave his full energy over to the church, now known by a new name. "Higher Dimensions" was a name fraught with legal entanglements and implications. In the bankruptcy proceedings, Pastor Carlton and the church had lost legal ownership of its creative property. A name change seemed less complicated than untangling the legal matters related to remaining "Higher Dimensions." So, the little church that had begun in Jenks, Oklahoma had refreshed its identity yet again. What started as Higher Dimensions Evangelistic Center in the 1980s and then became Higher Dimensions Family Church in the 1990s was, by 2006, "New Dimensions." And it was now to New Dimensions that Pastor Jesse gave his all, picking up the slack and filling in the gaps that numerous departures created. With his laptop under his arm and his Venti cup of Starbucks coffee in hand, Jesse seemed in constant motion, an unwavering bundle of optimism in even our bleakest moments. Until he wasn't.

It was March of 2008. At first, it was his hair that seemed noticeably different. Jesse always kept an artfully coiffed afro, perfectly lined, every jet-black, coily strand in place. We were having one of our Sunday afternoon services at Trinity Episcopal, singing praise and worship songs from our hearts. As refugees still with nowhere to go, we remained incredibly grateful for the hospitality of our Episcopalian hosts. Ever determined to put the most optimistic spin on our situation, Jesse bounded to the lectern to give his typically upbeat welcome to the small congregation. It was at that point that I noticed that the texture of his hair had become uncharacteristically silky; there were patches, new bald spots revealing scalp where his hair should have been.

The next week, Jesse returned to his usual role in the Sunday service, wearing a gray silk suit perfectly tailored to his slight frame. We went through the usual sequence of opening prayer, praise, and worship before Jesse rose to deliver the welcome as he always did. But something about his presence was different. There was an effort in his motion that none of us had ever seen before. As he approached the lectern, his motions were slow and deliberate, even labored. Where his afro had been, most of his hair was now involuntarily straight. Although his speech was noticeably slurred and incoherent, his dazzling smile worked hard to peer through. And whatever he was trying to say to the congregation made no sense. It was unsettling; startling, even.

The worship service continued, but all of us were distracted by this new and unfamiliar version of Jesse who, in his own way, was clearly crying for help. We all knew he ate poorly and lived on coffee. He worked around the clock and didn't know how to stop. He was suffering from exhaustion, maybe. Whatever the case, we knew he was in no condition to drive himself home that day.

I approached him after the service and called for James to take Jesse's car keys and drive him to his apartment. Jesse was too weak to protest. While James got Jesse home, I picked up something from Piccadilly Restaurant and soon met them both at the apartment. I thought he needed a decent dinner, and we stayed with him to make sure he ate every bite. But crumbs tumbled from either side of the fork that he struggled to hold in his trembling hand.

We contacted Pastor David and Nicole ("Niki") Ogundare, Pastor Carlton's executive assistant, as this seemed more than a simple case of exhaustion or malnourishment. Pastor David had noticed the changes and also expressed concern. He'd also been to Jesse's apartment to check in on him. Through the shrinking of our church, through all the daggers hurled at us by the Christian press, and through the loss of our building and our property, Jesse had been our good-humored, unwavering light. He was always full of optimism and hope, always ready to bound forward and praise God with all his heart, soul, mind, and strength. I had never even known Jesse to have so much as a stuffy nose or a head cold. And now this.

Jesse's twin sister, Andrea, flew to Tulsa to check on him. A musical force in her own right, Andrea was a magnificent soloist. Specifically for her visit, our choir rehearsed a song, for which she would sing lead on the forthcoming service. The lyrics of the song were all about trying times that cause us to look inward and encourage ourselves to strengthen our own faith. If anything could energize and restore Jesse, it would be the sound of his sister's angelic voice.

Andrea was welcomed warmly and sang her heart out on that Sunday morning as we all knew that she would. Jesse seemed revived with her visit and beamed with pride as she held forth, singing with vigor and conviction under the anointing of the Holy Ghost. For a moment, we were shifted into a place of reassurance. We felt encouraged. Everything would be alright.

But the hope was short-lived. Soon after, Jesse had a relapse and was hospitalized at St. Francis in Tulsa. Short-term treatments gave him enough energy for a brief rebound, but the doctors there never got to the root of the problem.

CHAPTER 18

"Our normal was no longer the same..."

– Cassandra

T he year was 2008. It brought a whirlwind of changes, both personal and otherwise. Biblically, the number "eight" is associated with new beginnings, new orders, or new creations. Seasons that bring new beginnings, however, can also mark profound endings.

In 2008, my employer, Verizon Communications, resumed its third round of layoffs; 2008 was my year to be cut. That same year, my ex-husband, who was also a friend and the father of my daughter, was found dead at his workplace. He had been employed there for thirty years as a chemical engineer. My only living uncle died in 2008. It was a period of great loss but also a time for me to realize just how far I'd come. None of these losses devastated me. Instead, I found a strength within that I knew came from my deep understanding about God and about myself. Nearly a decade earlier, my healing began when I listened repeatedly to Bishop Pearson's sermon titled, *The God Who is Able*. That sermon took deep root in my spirit and strengthened me to the point that I became unbreakable. Did I cry a few tears? Of course, I did. But by 2008, I was an entirely new person, light years beyond the dark place where I found myself when my parents died. I had come to know God as my sustainer, and that sustainer lived within me.

The Higher Dimensions Choir, once mighty in number and reputation, was now the New Dimensions Chorale. Since meeting at Trinity, we had continued to rehearse and sing at regular services, as well as at a few functions here and there. With our few voices, we recorded our last CD with Bishop Pearson, titled *After the Rain*. There were no hand-clapping, foot-stomping, soul-stirring tracks on that project. Instead, it was more meditative, more reflective. We did not go to the Church Studio as with prior projects. Instead, a sound engineer brought his equipment to the Trinity sanctuary, where we donned our headphones on the chancel. We sang under Pastor David's direction, taking brief breaks as we needed on the stone steps of the altar. Appropriately, one of the numbers that Bishop Pearson recorded on that project was his own rendition of *Everything Must Change*. Nothing could have been more true at that particular time.

We continued holding Sunday services at Trinity Episcopal Church. In the early months of 2008, however, Bishop Pearson presented the idea of moving our congregation to All Souls

Unitarian Church. The senior minister there was Reverend Marlin Lavanhar. Bishop Pearson and Reverend Lavanhar met in 2001 to debate President G.W. Bush's federal funding of faith-based initiatives from opposite sides. After Bishop Pearson's theological shift began, he and Reverend Lavanhar became close friends. Reverend Lavanhar saw that Bishop Pearson's message resonated with classic Universalism. I remember the awkward feeling I had when Bishop Pearson mentioned the move to All Souls. I felt unsettled by the very thought of moving from one place to yet another place that was not our home. That's when it hit me: our normal was no longer the same, and I wasn't sure that it would ever be again. So, I chose to focus on the fact that we were the same group of people, regardless of where we met for worship. That thought made the conditions tolerable for me.

Bishop Pearson often said that Reverend Lavanhar was a kind spirit and a brilliant thinker. It was clear that he had made a new friend when we started to hear Reverend Lavanhar's name in the weekly service. We soon received an official invitation from All Souls Church. Bishop Pearson was scheduled to speak there; the New Dimensions Chorale would also sing.

When we arrived, I noticed that the church practically had an all-white congregation. As far as I could tell, there may have been three or four people of color who were All Souls members at that time. The service that we attended was welcoming. The people were warm and friendly, and they seemed to enjoy our presence. We knew nothing about the Unitarian Universalist tradition at that time. As with all of our invitations, however, we went because we were committed to the ministry, and we felt that helping to usher in the presence of God through music was our way of giving.

In June of 2008, we left Trinity. We expressed gratitude for their hospitality for the prior two and a half years. At the invitation of Reverend Lavanhar, the New Dimensions congregation moved to the All Souls church building where we began having our own Sunday morning services there at 11:30. We definitely appreciated the spaces that Trinity and All Souls each gave us to meet for worship. With the move to All Souls, we gained a newfound appreciation for good acoustics. It's amazing the difference a facility can make. Yet, each move was like trying to get comfortable in clothing that is neither yours nor fits.

It was clear to me that Bishop Pearson felt obligated to find a place where New Dimensions could worship without feeling like outcasts because of his theological shift. I can't speak for everyone else, but I never felt like that was his responsibility. As always, however, Bishop Pearson was more focused on us and making sure we were okay than he was on himself.

There were other important beginnings in 2008. My oldest grandson, Terrance McClellan II, turned eight years old and I celebrated my forty-eighth birthday. That year, my son won full custody of his ten-month-old daughter, Terran, who brought unspeakable joy and light to our family.

Bishop Pearson's book, *The Gospel of Inclusion*, was finished in 2006, but was first available in 2008. That year, a single bookstore, Barnes & Noble in South Tulsa, agreed to carry it. In it, he presented all of the details and explanations related to his message. It contained the answers to many questions that people had, questions that, too often, were camouflaged as hateful reactions to his heresy. But, there was a thirst for understanding. For anyone who wanted clarity on where Bishop Pearson stood, *The Gospel of Inclusion* afforded a deep probe into the scriptures. It offered a close examination of words that appear in the Bible, their original meanings, and their translations. In the book, he explains, for example, the various translations of the word *hell* and how many of our modern Christian concepts derive from a combination of different belief systems. *The Gospel of Inclusion* grapples with the self-contradictions in Evangelical thought and offers the hope of a God who really and truly loves all.

One particular new beginning seemed to eclipse all of the news of that year for us. It was June of 2008. A relative newcomer to the political scene secured enough delegates to become the presumptive nominee of the Democratic Party for the 2008 presidential election. He was a young senator from Illinois with a strange name. But he spoke of hope and change with spark and charisma and true conviction. And he was black. His name was Barack Obama.

For all of the rainy days in the life of New Dimensions, this became our sunshine. We were elated over the possibility of having the nation's first African American president! There was a fresh energy in the air, and people of color felt a kind of hope we'd never experienced before. It was like a dream, something we never imagined we would see in our lifetime. It seemed to symbolize the breaking of every mental shackle that had ever held us down. We felt almost schizophrenic, as we were torn between two extremely opposite realities. Simultaneously, we were both overjoyed at the prospect of a President Barack Obama, and silently grieving the loss of our church.

CHAPTER 19

"We were terminally ill. We would die."

– Teresa

"The sense of uncertainty took its toll."

– Cassandra

E arly in the summer of 2008, we left Trinity Episcopal. However, our time there gave us the opportunity to see a side of humanity that is often invisible to the Evangelical world. Instead of expecting the homeless, hungry, and hurting to come to us, our time at Trinity gave us an opportunity to go to them. We had no great religious spectacle to offer them—no more mega-church amenities, no big choir, no books or CDs, or DVDs, or A-list celebrities. We had nothing to offer them except our presence, our humility, and our love. I look back on the Trinity days with gratitude, not just for the generosity of their congregation, but for the opportunity to see that the homeless and poor are not just abstract concepts. They are real people who care very little about systems of belief; instead, they simply want to know that they matter.

There was a white stone church with a steeple that I had passed often whenever I headed south on Peoria Ave. Several of my university colleagues attended there, and although I knew they called themselves Unitarians, I never gave much thought to their doctrinal leanings. The exterior of All Souls Unitarian Church was all white, and its congregation was nearly equally so. Nestled among evergreens in one of Tulsa's more elite zip codes, All Souls was a generations-old haven of liberal ideology and free thinking. Founded in 1921, the year of the Tulsa Race Massacre, All Souls had a history of courageous political activism. Its long-time senior minister, Dr. John Wolfe, made headlines when he took a stand for civil rights at a time when very few white men dared to. His successor, Reverend Lavanhar, was set to welcome the New Dimensions outcasts by midyear in 2008. The timing could not have been more divinely ordered.

Beginning in June 2008, we borrowed the All Souls sanctuary and worshipped there—the hundred or so that remained—as an autonomous New Dimensions congregation. The sanctuary, which could seat around five hundred, was much smaller than either our former church on Memorial Drive or Trinity. And the acoustics were much better than at Trinity. It was the tradition of All Souls to hold a single, early Sunday service throughout the summer months, which meant that their building was unused from 11:00am on. So we began to have our own Sunday morning services there at 11:30. Pastor Carlton would often preach, but Pastor Jesse, whose strength would come and go, would sometimes minister when he felt up to it. By this time, Pastor Carlton was occupied with thoughts of supporting his family. It was clear that his following had dwindled and his options and resources in Tulsa had dried up. He was now officially branded a heretic and shunned by all who might have offered him the help he needed to recover. The Bible Belt of the country had nothing left to offer him. He was looking elsewhere.

The timing of our move to All Souls coincided with the heat of the 2008 presidential campaign. Barack Obama had won the Democratic nomination, and there was a sense stirring in the air that he just might become the first African American president of the United States. In Tulsa, Oklahoma, with its long legacy of troubled race relations and its unwavering, collective conservative mindset, the prospect of a black man in the Oval Office was absolutely terrifying. But for our small band of New Dimensions heretics and many of the liberal Unitarians who lent us their space, it was the most exciting thing imaginable!!

Unitarians, I came to understand, are distinguished by their ability to regard multiple religious perspectives at once without pledging absolute allegiance to any one doctrinal stance in particular. So the church welcomes people of various faiths—from atheists, to agnostics, to Buddhists, and others— while emphasizing community over belief. Although the church included both conservatives and liberals, both

Christians and non-Christians, Reverend Lavanhar went out of his way to show support to Pastor Carlton and to welcome our predominantly black, Pentecostal-Inclusionist cohort to its building.

As the summer months passed, I felt the need to cling to what was left of my church family as though we were the last survivors on the quickly-sinking Titanic. August was coming, which meant that All Souls would reclaim the 11:30am worship time. It was no secret that Pastor Carlton had job offers out of the state, including one in Chicago. Up until that point, Higher Dimensions had been able to survive in some form, even though each new phase diminished us further. With All Souls resuming its regular worship schedule and with Pastor Carlton set to transplant his family elsewhere, all signs indicated one thing: with no Pastor Carlton and no place to call our own, the church originally known as Higher D would be extinguished altogether. We were terminally ill; we would die.

Although it certainly felt like a death to us, from another perspective, we were fused with, or absorbed by, All Souls. Bill Sherman, a reporter with the *Tulsa World*, did a feature on the story. He quoted what Reverend Lavanhar told his congregation: "It is truly historic. Nothing quite like this has ever happened before . . . And it comes at a time when it seems like our entire nation is entering a new era . . . [when] 'the next president of the United States may very well be African American."

The transitions from Higher Dimensions to Trinity and then to All Souls were hard and fast. Our name was "New Dimensions," but we still felt tethered to our Higher Dimensions past and remained inextricably linked to that identity. Each move gave us the sense of losing our home one day, and waking up in a homeless shelter the next day. The welcoming committee at All Souls was nothing less than warm and inviting; their sentiments, however, were not shared by the entire congregation. As we grappled with our place at All Souls, Reverend Lavanhar and his pastoral team extended to us a love and acceptance that was beyond belief. For many others, however, the sudden presence of this black contingent of worshippers with their loud, Pentecostal music was confusing and off-putting. Never in its eighty-plus years of existence had the All Souls congregation had to contend with loud drums, moving bodies, and singing drenched in raw emotion and spirit. Reverend Lavanhar and his assistant, Reverend Tamara Lebak, graciously invited us to bring our whole selves to their church. But for many, our undiluted blackness was an uncomfortable culture shock.

We had a choice. We could either live in the disappointment and the hurt from the past, or we could move forward. We'd come to the realization that people we once called friends could easily flip the script; the only choice was to move forward, believing it would all somehow work in our favor.

We managed to make the best of things. Yet, there

remained hope for a change that would somehow get us back to a place of our own. Bishop Pearson, like us, was now also without a church home. While he remained in Tulsa, he attended All Souls each Sunday when not speaking out of town. He wasn't an active part of the staff at that time. It was odd and awkward to see him and Gina sitting in the pews on Sundays, not on an elevated chancel. It was a mental adjustment we all had to make.

The last day of our existence as the Higher Dimensions church family was August 31, 2008. There was a certain irony in that day. There were plenty of tears and there was much reflection as we held our last Sunday service. Immediately afterward, however, our choir was scheduled to sing at the grand opening of the newly constructed jewel of the city, the Bank of Oklahoma Arena in downtown Tulsa. This nineteen-thousand-seat, multi-purpose facility was the largest of its kind in the area, outranking even the Mabee Center. New Dimensions Chorale accompanied pop recording artist and native Oklahoman, Sam Harris, providing the background vocals to Sam's original song titled *Change is on the Way*. Unbeknownst to Sam, there couldn't have been a more fitting song to describe that particular moment of our lives.

Those last few years of trying to hold on to our church were exhausting. It was just as exhausting trying to get accustomed to our new normal. Things were awkward to say the least. The sense of uncertainty took its toll. The need to constantly explain ourselves also took its toll. The fact that we no longer had our own facility didn't stop the comments or inquiries from coming. In fact, they may have even increased during this season. People wanted to know our real feelings about the loss and our real feelings about Bishop Pearson since the loss. Some people approached us to recruit us to their churches; others were still interested in debating. And then there were those who took pleasure in reminding us that our loss would not have happened had Bishop Pearson remained true to the Gospel. So many of those conversations ended with us somehow having to defend our stance. Eventually, some of us refrained from having those conversations at all. Although we truly wanted people to understand things clearly rather than jump to their own conclusions, it was so draining. At that point, some of us just needed space to regroup, reflect, and gather ourselves, even if that meant staying at home every Sunday and attending no church at all.

CHAPTER 20

"And then, in the wee hours, the phone rang..."

– Cassandra

Eventually, Pastor Jesse would hand over Bishop Pearson's social media responsibilities to me to manage. He now served in a new capacity, since Bishop Pearson was no longer operating as a Senior Minister. Pastor Jesse also continued singing and assisting Pastor David Smith with the New Dimensions Chorale while coping with his illness, the seriousness of which no one knew at the time.

The last major event that Pastor Jesse and I collaborated on was the Converging Faiths Leadership Summit, hosted by Bishop Pearson and held in Atlanta, Georgia in September of 2008. I served alongside Pastor Jesse, helping with organization, logistics, communications, and so forth. The purpose of the conference was to begin organizing an interdenominational fellowship of churches, ministries and/or ministers who were interested in Inclusion. Together with

Nicole Ogundare, Bishop Pearson's executive assistant, we began preparing for the event from Tulsa and flew to Georgia the week of the event. Invited guest presenters were D.E. Paulk, Bishop Yvette Flunder, Harold Lovelace, David Alexander, Rabbi James Levinson, Barbara King, and Michael Beckwith.

Pastor Jesse still wore many hats, but his primary function was to assist Bishop Pearson, as he usually did. But this time, something was different about him. Something seemed a little off about his demeanor. He arrived later than expected which was very unusual, as he was always known for his punctuality. He was also somewhat disoriented, even forgetful, and appeared fatigued. To those of us who knew him well, it was obvious that something was going on. We completed our mission in Atlanta and closed out the four-day summit and returned safely to Tulsa.

Pastor Jesse's condition worsened. It was time to contact his family. Between Pastor David, Niki, and Pastor Carlton, the necessary calls and arrangements were made. Jesse's father drove up from Orlando, Florida to collect his ailing son. By the winter of that year, we got news that the diagnosis was Lymphoma.

The backdrop of all of the twists and turns of that year was the anticipation of the presidential election. On election night, Pastor David excused us from our usual Tuesday evening choir rehearsal. We all rushed home to our televisions to watch the minute-by-minute coverage of the election returns.

As each state reported its electoral outcome, a sense of anticipation marked November 4, 2008 as a day of unprecedented celebration. Then it happened! Senator Barack Hussein Obama, II of Illinois was elected the nation's first African-American president of the United States, beating Senator John McCain of Arizona. There were no words to fully express what we felt inside. It was all so surreal. It gave us hope.

It was in the early morning hour of December 13th when I received the news from Nicole. She had gone to Florida to check on Jesse and remained there visiting with him and his family. Nicole and I had talked earlier that evening about his condition. And then, in the wee hours, the phone rang:
"He's gone," she said.

December 13th was the three-hundred-forty-eighth day of the year 2008. Our true Prince of Worship, Pastor Jesse Williams, Jr. passed away in the home of a family member in Florida.

Upon hearing Nicole's words, I slowly hung up the phone. I took a deep breath, closed my eyes, and in a small whisper, called out his name. It was around 3am, and I proceeded to call other members of the New D. Chorale. Our beloved Pastor Jesse earned his wings. He took flight, transitioning from this earth right in the middle of our church transition, just before the oath of office was administered to President Elect Barack Obama.

CHAPTER 21

"The commitment at All Souls is to love beyond belief."

– Cassandra

In 2009, we learned that Bishop Pearson and his family were leaving Tulsa for Chicago. He had accepted a position there as interim minister at Christ Universal Temple. For me, this was the end of the line at All Souls Church. I couldn't see myself remaining in this strange land after his departure. My mind was made up, and I planned to leave All Souls as soon as he left Tulsa. But before that could happen, Bishop Pearson called a meeting with the New D. Chorale, inviting us to his home one evening for dinner.

He explained that his intentions were to speak and teach the good news of the Gospel of Inclusion; this "New Thought" church in Chicago would be a stepping stone, helping him to accomplish that. His real reason for the meeting, however, was to remind us of who we were as the New Dimensions Chorale. He reminded us of our roles as singers and worshippers. Since the days of South Memorial Drive, nothing about that had changed. Our voices were still instruments of the Holy Spirit, and as ministers, our role was to stand before the people singing our songs to help usher in the presence of God. From the meeting that night, I was reaffirmed in my purpose as a member of the New D Chorale. I remembered my own healing at Higher D a decade or so earlier, and knew that I could use my voice to connect other hurting people with that Divine Presence. That meeting changed my course, and I had faith in Pastor David Smith's leadership. I decided to remain a member of the New Dimensions Chorale at All Souls Church.

After Bishop Pearson moved to Chicago, the New D Chorale made an all-out effort to embrace its new reality. Once we became permanent fixtures at All Souls, it became crystal clear that we brought more diversity than some could handle. We had infiltrated their camp, and there were moments when we were just as uncomfortable with it as they were. Our loyalty to the New Dimensions group, however, was the reason we decided to stay. These initial experiences at All Souls took me back, way back, to what I felt as a child in Sand Springs, Oklahoma. I was the only black child trying to fit in on the school bus and in the classroom with all white children. It had been forty years since I'd felt like such an outsider. It was a hard pill to swallow in the twenty-first century; it was even harder to believe that I felt this way inside of a church. Sometimes, I wondered if Bishop Pearson ever considered that we would face this kind of challenge.

I recognized it as the season we were in, so I found purpose in the struggle. Barack Obama would become the first African American President. I viewed my presence at All Souls as a way of doing my part to create the right kind of change in America. Being tolerated by white people was nothing new for me. I survived it as a kid, and I was familiar with it as an adult. I completely understood that our presence interrupted their sense of normalcy. I also understood that there were things about our worship style—including our constant references to Jesus and to God—that were unwelcomed reminders of the religious institutions that many of these Unitarians thought they had escaped. Some openly resisted our presence, making clear their intent to keep All Souls the way it had always been. When that didn't happen, some of the All Souls members left the church. Over time, a few more of the New Dimensions members left as well. They'd already been in one battle. They were tired of fighting.

To our pleasant surprise, Reverend Lavanhar proactively addressed the issue of race relations head-on. Together with ministers and staff, he made it a priority at All Souls. He hired an African-American intercultural consultant to help us all navigate through the adjustment period. It surprised me to see their concentrated effort to bring awareness and build bridges across our differences. It was something I'd never witnessed in a church setting before.

Reverend Marlin insisted that everyone remain at the table

and it wasn't based on all of us seeing eye to eye. That statement had a profound effect on me and allowed me to understand my purpose there. With time, effort, and training, I witnessed some hearts and minds changing right before my eyes. I also witnessed my own personal growth in understanding the LGBTQ community and the Unitarian Universalist beliefs and practices.

All Souls Church is a work in progress, committed to becoming as racially, culturally, and generationally diverse as possible. I believe they are well on their way. Their willingness to make space at the table for New Dimensions was a great testament to me. They've courageously spoken out on complex issues, and they are committed to fighting for what is fair, regardless of whose side they must take. They demonstrate a genuine belief in Inclusion. God couldn't have given me a more interesting place to learn from, or a more open-minded leader to follow during that season of racial tension across America. Reverend Lavanhar often reminds us that "at All Souls, we are much more interested in what you do and less concerned about what you say you believe." The commitment at All Souls is to love beyond belief.

CHAPTER 22

"I recalled what Bishop Veron Ashe said..."

– Cassandra

In December 2005, NPR aired its episode titled "Heretic" on *This American Life*. At that time, our shrinking congregation was facing bankruptcy and foreclosure on our property. In 2006, while we were worshipping at Trinity, we were too absorbed in our own survival to realize that our story was making its way around the world. Lisa Bonet's brief visit to Tulsa to explore the possibility of producing our story as a movie was fascinating for us, but soon forgotten. We finished our time at Trinity, then transitioned to All Souls in 2008, unaware of the widespread interest in Bishop Pearson and the Gospel of Inclusion.

In 2010, we received an official announcement: indeed, a movie was in the works! A feature-length film was being made about the excommunication of Bishop Pearson, and it was based on the 2005 NPR feature. Initially titled *"Heretic,"* the movie would tell the story of the rise and fall of Bishop

Pearson and the series of events that led to the loss of our church. Shortly after the movie was announced, the scriptwriter traveled to Tulsa to interview the group of us who chose to go the distance with Bishop Pearson. We later learned that the movie would be a Netflix original with the potential to reach tens of millions of Netflix subscribers, on their laptops, iPads, smartphones, and in their homes. I recalled what Bishop Veron Ashe said in his prophecy from the year 2000: ". . . Strange television." Indeed!

It became clear to me that the message of Inclusion would reach the masses despite the obstacles that once stood in the way. The Gospel of Inclusion was bigger than all of us. The experiences that we shared because of it ensured that we would never be the same.

In 2011, Bishop Pearson left the position of interim minister at Christ Universal Temple. The *Chicago Tribune* headline read "Christ Universal Temple Leader Stepping Down." The article quoted Bishop Pearson as saying, "I was trying to extend the church message beyond the church walls to an inclusive audience . . . but they want to take the church in a different direction, back to where they were before I got there."[1]

When we heard the news, those of us who remained together at All Souls Church had high hopes that he would return to Tulsa right away, but that didn't happen. He remained in Chicago for another three years. In addition to fulfilling a schedule of speaking engagements, Bishop Pearson began a monthly service for his Chicago followers, frequently flying back to Tulsa to check on the wellbeing of his parents. Dad Pearson's health began to decline in 2014, and it was in that year that Bishop Pearson returned to Tulsa. He became an affiliate minister of All Souls and began speaking on the third Sunday of each month.

On March 21, 2015, Dad Pearson left us. Adam Louis Pearson, the beloved grandfather of Higher Dimensions, passed away two days after Bishop Pearson's sixty-second birthday. Remembering my own feelings when my dad passed away, I was sensitive to his and prayed that he could process his heartache without getting stuck in a dark place.

The memorial service for Dad Pearson was held in Tulsa at Transformation Church, formerly Greenwood Christian Center. Transformation Church is now pastored by Michael Todd, who grew up at Higher Dimensions. We all gathered there to sing, fellowship, and celebrate the life of Dad Pearson. His memorial service was made even more memorable because we were together again as a church family.

In 2016, there was a casting call for extras for the movie about Bishop Pearson's theological shift, now titled *Come Sunday*. The call was posted online for those in the Atlanta area where the film was being made. Soon, the buzz about the movie was everywhere. Bishop Pearson was hired as a consultant on the set. On one occasion, while delivering his Sunday message, he mentioned how he could feel the anointing of God while on the set during particular scenes. He talked about the pain that resurfaced, as well as the therapy and healing he experienced as he watched the story unfold. Netflix announced the official release date of April 13, 2018, but it seemed to take forever to come. The weekend before the official release date, a special screening was held at Tulsa's Circle Cinema to a sold-out audience.

1.Brachear, Manya. "Christ Universal Temple Leader Stepping Down." *Chicago Tribune*, 3 Jan. 2011.

CHAPTER 23

"That seat, in that place, at that moment, was like pure gold."

                                   – Teresa

It's been eighteen years since Bishop Veron Ashe gave the prophecy foretelling the fate of our Pastor and our church. And it's been sixteen years since Carlton Pearson proved that the quickest way to empty a church is to preach God's all-inclusive love. At its prime, Higher Dimensions church was electric. It had the best musicians, the best choir for miles around, the most flamboyant hats, the shiniest rhinestones, and the most fashionable parishioners. It was the regular stomping ground of the biggest Christian celebrities and gospel artists in the world, and on any given Sunday, any one of them might drop in to regale the congregation with a song or two. It also had a rock-star-status pastor undergoing a crisis of consciousness, a severe mental disconnect between the hell-fire and brimstone that he preached and the expansive love that he felt for God's people—all of God's people.

Within months of sharing his new revelation from the pulpit, the once-spectacular Higher D began to lose both members and money. But some of us stuck around to support Pastor Carlton, to ask more questions, and to learn more of what this notion of "inclusion" was all about. And the more we learned, the more we came to realize how little we actually knew about the world beyond our own religious walls.

A wise person said that if the map and the road disagree, by all means, dismiss the map and trust the road. For too long, Evangelical Christianity has been the map of an imaginary reality, strangely misaligned with the actual road of life that most of us human beings travel. The real road is full of pitfalls, trials, and temptations that can take us down a few pegs, reminding us of our fragile humanity despite the sanctimonious veneer we may claim.

In the years since Pastor Carlton was first declared a heretic, the Christian world has been shaken with a series of unsavory headlines. In 2006, Evangelical giant Ted Haggard made national news for cheating on his wife with a gay male prostitute. In 2008, a parking-lot fist-fight between Prophetess Juanita Bynum and her then husband, Thomas Weeks, led to an arrest and assault charge. In 2009, the son of Bishop T.D. Jakes was accused of exposing himself to an undercover Dallas police officer. His daughter later became pregnant at thirteen years old. In 2010, Atlanta megachurch pastor and anti-gay activist Bishop Eddie Long was sued by a third alleged male victim for sexual abuse. In 2012, Evangelist Richard Roberts, son of the legendary Oral Roberts, was arrested for DUI. That same year, megachurch pastor Creflo Dollar was arrested on a battery charge after a family dispute. Also in 2012, administrative members of Victory Christian Center in Tulsa were charged with failing to report the alleged rape of a thirteen-year-old girl on church property. To these unfortunate events can be added the many accusations of sexual abuse against priests in the Catholic Church.[1]

This is all now historical fact—not theory, not conjecture, and not opinion or fabrication. And none of this is cause for any sort of finger-pointing celebration; instead, this simply proves the point that the Christian Club is no more exempt from sin—and certainly no less in need of unconditional love—than the Hindu, the Atheist, or the openly gay man who is brave enough to live the truth of his identity. Evangelical Christianity is a map drawn with good intentions pointing to unattainable ideals; it is too obsolete, however, to match the road of life that real people travel. The Christian label does very little to exempt us from our human frailty. We all fall down. We all need God.

Just as Bishop Ashe foretold, Pastor Carlton and Higher Dimensions paid a dear price for preaching the heart of an all-inclusive, all-loving God. The church lost its building and all of its property and struggled along for years before officially dissolving in 2008. The building at 8621 S. Memorial is now owned by another thriving ministry, and a Christian school now occupies much of the space that once housed our church. But Pastor Carlton's story continues to unfold.

In April 2018, Netflix released its original feature film, *Come Sunday*, which depicts Pastor Carlton's journey from Evangelical Superstar to inclusive heretic. Cassandra and I were at the Tulsa premiere of the film, which played to a sold-out crowd. In this crowd were many former members of Higher D, people we hadn't worshipped with, in some cases, in over a decade. It was painful, yet good to see them. In a bittersweet moment of irony, the movie brought us all together again—blacks, whites, Native Americans, former Catholics, former Lutherans. And there were others there with us—Unitarians, Atheists, gays, and transsexuals—all gathered to see this story of spiritual awakening and transformation, of painful loss, and the hope that only the purest love can bring. For some, the story itself was unfamiliar and new. But for many, this fictional depiction of the marvel that was Higher Dimensions was like traveling back in time to revisit the clapping hands, the swaying bodies, and the singing voices of people we shared life with before our church was fragmented and dissolved.

It was nearly time. In the black-box theatre, the anticipation we felt was palpable. A remaining few rushed in, quickly claiming the last of the empty seats. The lights were lowered and the auditorium grew dark. A holy hush fell over the audience. Late arriving? Slow parking? Too bad. That seat, in that place, at that moment, was like pure gold. Once seated, we dared not move.   James and I held hands, interlocking our fingers, our heartbeats suspended.   The audience held its breath. The screen lit up and the film began to roll. And there we were, back again at that fiery, sacred space we once called home.

---

1. Most of the stories cited here made national news; all are easily verifiable online.

POSTLUDE

Cassandra's Reflection

You can argue the script, but you can't argue the experience. In the middle of a paradigm shift, Bishop Pearson was labeled a heretic for presenting a radically inclusive God and deemphasizing a mythological hell. Sharing these thoughts with his church caused a kind of hell for him and his family right here on earth, and a ripple effect was felt throughout the congregation. His personal loss was massive. His personal gain, however, was a new perspective, a new vision and version of God. He found an all-inclusive God, one beyond our religious trappings and cultural conditioning. His pain birthed the Gospel of Inclusion, and his story became the basis of numerous articles, a book, a radio feature, and a movie. Although his original focus was intended to be the vast love of God, the topic that ignites most conversations is his rejection of the belief in a literal hell. Unapologetically, Bishop Pearson continues to evolve in his newfound freedom.

The Gospel of Inclusion has been dissected from every angle by its detractors. Many seem fixated on disproving its validity, some even simply for argument's sake. But the Gospel of Inclusion allows for the infinite potential of an all-loving God, minus the requirement of hell.

If you're stuck behind religion, you may not realize that there is a gateway to broader thinking. There is freedom in the realization that the Source of all things is a God of infinite creativity and possibility. This realization is a bridge from the limitations of religion to the freedom of knowing and cultivating your own relationship with Divinity. There is no formula to follow before crossing that bridge; what happens afterward depends on what you experience as a free agent in your higher consciousness.

When I was in my dark place, unsure if I'd ever recover from my grief, I found myself sitting *beneath a heretic's wings* each Sunday. The words he spoke came from a place that my soul recognized, but my mind had forgotten. Those were the words that reminded me of who I was and helped me to heal from the inside out. It wasn't a quick fix, but a process over time. That process kept me true to my covering, committed to the ministry, and coming back for more. I learned that when the light goes out in your life, it's dark, and darkness looks the same to everyone who's in it. The difference between you and the other person in the dark is the circumstances that put you there. By the time Bishop Pearson entered his dark place, I was free and healed of mine. It was only natural that I would remain in place under his leadership and offer my support to the support system that helped restore me back to life.

I got to experience the unfolding of a new idea. I got to watch the owner of that idea survive various stages that I didn't recognize at the time. Once that experience was documented and named, then I could see it as a movement. This was no external movement, however; instead, it was a spiritual movement, already inside of me. And this confirmed to me that I was in the right place at the right time.

As I reflect on this experience, I am filled with gratitude to have grown beyond the restrictions of my preconditioned mind. I have evolved to know what it means to be free and independent from traditional, religious, stagnant thinking. I am grateful that I was stretched to accept the infallible love of God.

Teresa and I are part of the remnant of Tulsa's Higher Dimensions. We were there to witness the rise, fall, and new birth of Bishop Pearson. And through the series of events surrounding that experience, our own minds and hearts have expanded to know that there is more and there will always be more. Because our Source is infinite, there is no end to knowledge. Knowing is within us, and transcending is the natural order of things. When we don't trust what we know, we argue about what we believe.

All any of us are really trying to do is find our way in a life we've not lived before. We occupy a body that won't last forever; we think with a mind that's subject to change with our changing awareness of God. I spent the first half of my life looking for something to make me feel complete. This half of my life, I am convinced that I've had it all along. It has become crystal clear that my life was assigned to me, to manage, to nourish, and to interpret as I am enlightened by the light within me. I am humbled to have this privilege.

~~~~~~~~~~~~~~~~~~

Teresa's Reflection

~~~~~~~~~~~~~~~~~~

I miss my Higher Dimensions family and I always will. From time to time, I still see them in passing—at the grocery store, at the mall, at the Y. Theologically speaking, many are exactly where they were eighteen years ago, and I respect their right to remain in their comfort zones. The release of *Come Sunday* has sparked a fresh round of vitriol and debate. The same arguments, the same accusations, the same name-calling, scripture-quoting, combative voices are raging in much the same way as they did in 2002. But now, there are also new questions and opportunities for new dialogue about this mystery called the Love of God. Thanks to the marvel of Netflix, the conversation is worldwide and ongoing.

Pastor Carlton liberated me to ask questions, and I have been doing so ever since he first dared to broach those startling questions of his own. The more I dig, the more I learn. The more I understand about the history and evolution of the Bible, the more I see it as distinct and separate from the God that I worship, the God whose love transcends traditions, creeds, and writings. Love is only love if it transcends, consistently, unconditionally, and inclusively.

Our pain and our loss—none of that matters to me now. A thick and impenetrable scab has formed over the place where my heart once hurt. Even though many still call me a heretic and a reprobate, I don't hold that against them. In fact, I understand their perspective completely, as I once had that very mindset. These are my brothers and my sisters— sincere, devout, precious, and beautiful people—and I still love them.

Scores of ministries were birthed out of Higher Dimensions. Every minister who ventured away from Higher D to further the Kingdom of God received Pastor Carlton's blessing. However, many of those pastors and evangelists (they know who they are) found it necessary to expunge any mention of Carlton Pearson's name from their marketing materials. Yet, nothing can erase the history we shared, the songs we sang, and the prayers we once prayed together. Anyone with a connection to Higher Dimensions will always be a part of the story of my life. More importantly, they are included in God's embrace. That will never change.

Right now, at this very moment, somewhere in the world, a fearful, restless soul is facing another sleepless night. She kneels to pray, feeling uncertain and unworthy, but hoping for divine reassurance. Strangely, she is compelled to get online and log in to her Netflix account. There, she finds a film about a preacher from Oklahoma who dared to declare the relentless love of God, a God who doesn't care if she's Christian, or Hindu, or Jewish, or Atheist, or lesbian, or labelled in any other way. This God, she finds, is pure, unstoppable, inclusive love. If millions like her can find hope and healing in this love, then the journey foretold by Bishop Veron Ashe was well worth it. Because love never fails, the story is far from over. The best is yet to come.

Index

(The page numbers in Index represents the print page number and will differ with the eBook page numbers. Page numbers in *italics* indicate photographs.)

African Americans, 9; church rituals of, 9; See also Black churches

After the Rain, "Everything Must Change" single, 206

albums: drop of album sales, 118; recording of, 56-57

All Souls Unitarian Church, 206, 207; demographics at, 207, 213-214; descriptions of, 212; founding of, 212; New Dimensions Chorale singing at, 207-208; New Dimensions membership at, 208, 213; service times at, 212; tension of denominations at, 215, 225

apostasy, 150,152

Ashe, Vernon, x; appearance of, 3; death of, 7, 8n; prophetic utterance of, 3-7, 228, 231, 233; upbringing of, 2

Azusa Choir, 52-53, 117, 120; songs of, 53;

Azusa Christian Life School of Theology, 125; discontinuing of, 178

"School of Ministry", 177, 191

Azusa Conference, ix, 12, 42, 49, 51, 53-54, 149; speakers at Azusa, 55; the last conference, 115, 119, 121

Azusa Conference demographics: diversity of, 54; fewer in number, 120-121; size of, 50; the lines of, 54

Azusa Praise: We Cry Out, x, 57

Barak Obama, 209-210, 213; election night of, 220-221, 225

Barnes & Noble: selling of *The Gospel of Inclusion*, 209

Beneath a Heretic's Wings Postlude, 237-242

Bible-Belt Christianity, xiii, 213

Black churches: diversity of, 11; financial support of pastors, 168; non-denominational, 11; run like corporations, 11; structure of, 10; Sunday school attire at, 10; the black pastor, 85-86; traditions of, 93

Black community: mental illness, 76 81,82

Blake, J.A., ix

Bonet, Lisa, Hollywood Actress, 185, 227

Bryant, Jamal: counterargument against Pearson, 197

Carlton Pearson's Social Media
    Presence, 191-192, 198n
Catholics, 2, 12
Cayce, Edgar, 2,
celebrity preachers, 11
Charisma Magazine: "Black
    Pentecostal Group
    Denounces Carlton
    Pearson", 155n;
    "Controversy Clouds
    Pearson's Ministry", 148,
    155n; "Pearson's Gospel of
    Inclusion Stirs
    Controversy", 147-148,
    155n; "We Need Tough
    Love", 151, 155n; 2004
    article fueled fire, 150
Christ Universal Temple, xi
Christian Life School of Theology,
    x
Christmas Day, 178
Church of God in Christ (COGIC):
    association with Pearson,
    151; origins, 49-50;
    practices of, 50; tradition of
    raising funds, 167
"Church Studio"; equipment of, 56
Come Sunday, 227-228; casting
    calls for, 229 diversity
    influence of the film, 234;
    Q&A session about the
    film, *114*; release date, 230,
    234
Converging Faiths Leadership
    Summit, 219; guest
    speakers at, 220
Daugherty, Billy Joe: opposing
    Gospel of Inclusion, 149
DaVinci, Leonardo, 1

Davis, Byron: death of, 187; funeral,
    189
denominations, 2; Lutherans, 2
Episcopalians, 2
Evangelical: black megachurches,
    11; Christianity, 232; elite,
    50; establishment, 3, 181;
    superstar, xiii
False Prophet, 164
Flunder, Yvette, 164, 165, 220
Fruga, Alvin: Azusa, 52-53; 124
Gaines, Adrienne, 155n
generating funds at Higher D, 167,
    171, 174
geographical divide, in Tulsa, 47-48
Gillespie, Natalie Nichols, 155n
Gospel of Inclusion: "Book Signing
    Event", *109*; conversations
    about, 130-134, 138 185,
    196, 197; Evangelical
    Christianity and the
    LGBTQ community, 116;
    Netflix film about, 227-
    228; new demographic,
    158; play inspired by, 135-
    136; prophecy of, 3-7; *The
    Gospel of Inclusion* book
    release, 209
Gospel of Inclusion and Social
    Media, 192-196
Gospel of Inclusion Backlash 96-98,
    101, 128-129, 132-134,
    139-143, 151, 185; losing
    of tithes and offerings, 150;
    "The Dangers of Carlton
    Pearson's 'Doctrine of
    Inclusion'" article, 198n
Gospel of Inclusion Defense, 91, 93,
    94, 157; reaction of verbal

attacks, 99, 101, 136, 137, 140-146

Gospel Music Royalty, 166

Grady, J. Lee, 151, 155n

Greenwood Christian Center, 187, 188; blended funeral choir, 189; memorial service for Dad Pearson, 229; similarities with Higher Dimensions, 188

Haggard, Ted, 151, 184, 185; cheating scandal, 232

Harris, Sam: *Change is on the Way*, 216

Harvard University, v

Higher Dimensions: Altar Call at, 22-23; anointing at, 16; at its prime, 231; attraction of, 23; church mothers of, 15; cliques of, 59; "crazy", inappropriate women of, 60-61; diversity of, 12, 16, 25, 86; energy at, 69; family environment of, 24-25; negative opinions of, keeping normalcy, 153, 168, 178; known as Higher D, 17, 21, 24, 51; last service, 173; the last service at, 179; last Sunday service, 174, 178; losing diversity, 154-155; new demographic, 158; origins of, 12, 75; popular sayings at, 20; presence of God at, 19; prophecy of, 3-7, 8n; service times of, 12-13; songs at, 17, 18, 19, 165; spiritual growth at, 64-65

Higher Dimensions and the Gospel of Inclusion, decrease in congregation, 93-95, 157-158, 161; new doctrine, 71, 76, 82; reactions of the loss of church family from new doctrine, 100-102, 154; reactions of the new doctrine, 71-72, 83, 91-92, 94, 115, 127, 175; decrease in congregation, 93-95, 157-158, 161

Higher Dimensions' Financial Issues, building and property, 169, 170, 173; finances at, 20-21; financial troubles at, 153, 163-164, 168, 169, 171

Higher Dimensions' Ministries, choir and its appearance, 19, 42; choir auditions at, 13-14, 63; elite choir, 63, 124; ministerial staff at, 17, 86; ministries of, 12, 87

Holy Ghost: recording music, 57

Holy Spirit: the presence of, 3, 15, 158

Homosexuality and Religion: decrease in church members, 190; rejection of, 158-159; verbal attacks, 159

Hood, Terry, 149

Hurricane Katrina, 169, 170

Jack's Funeral Home, 10, 30; memory chapel, 77

Jackson, Fred, 167, 168

Jakes, T. D., and Pearson's doctrine, 148; at Azusa, 51

Joint College of African American
    Pentecostal, x, 130, 152
Lavanhar, Marlin, 207, 208, 212,
    214-215, 225
Lebak, Tamara, 215
Lexi Show, The, 196, 197
LGBTQ community and All Souls,
    226
LGBTQ community and Higher D,
    161; visit from Bishop
    Yvette Flunder, 164
Live at Azusa, ix
Live at Azusa 2, x, 117
Live at Azusa 3, x
Live at Azusa 4, x
Mabee Center, 54-55
Martin, Gene: gospel singer guest at
    conference, 115
McClellan, Cassandra L.: arrival at
    Higher Dimensions, 38;
    family and tragedies of, 27-
    38, 205; ministry service
    of, 62, 123; personal and
    church background of, 27,
    59, 67, 205, 208, 209, 224
McClellan, Cassandra "Closing
    Reflection", 237-240
McIntosh, Gary, 188
"money-hungry" pastors, 150, 152,
    153; recruiting tactics, 152
National Association of
    Evangelicals, 151
national public radio: "Heretic"
    episode, x, 184, 173 227;
    This American Life, x
NBC's *Dateline*: Carlton Pearson's
    doctrinal shift, 184
Netflix, vi, 227-228

"New Dimensions", 200, 215;
    burnout of members, 216,
    217
New Dimensions Chorale, 206, 216,
    223-224; reality after
    Pearson's departure, 224,
    225
New Year's Eve, 180
News on 6 (Tulsa), 149
Ogundare, Nicole, 202, 220
Oklahoma City bombing, ix
Open Door Refuge Church of God
    in Christ, 159
Oral Roberts University, ix; Azusa
    held at, 51, Evangelistic
    Association, ix; influence
    on Carlton Pearson, 22,
    151
Orthodox, 2
Pearson, Adam Louis (father), ix, xi,
    65; death of, 229; greetings
    of, 66; "Mom & Dad"
    Pearson, *103*
Pearson, Carlton and All Souls, 216;
    departure to Chicago,
    Illinois, 223; return to All
    Souls, 228-229
Pearson, Carlton and Higher
    Dimensions, "Farewell to
    Higher D", *104*;
    "Fellowship through
    prayer", 108; personal
    anecdotes of, 21, 67; last
    comments at the last
    Higher D service, 179-180;
    popularity of, 23, 49, 64,
    65, 87; sermons of, 41,
    206; "The Pastor and First
    Lady of Higher

Dimensions", *112*; vision for Higher D, 171

Pearson, Carlton and The Gospel of Inclusion, book release of *The Gospel of Inclusion*, 209; branded as a heretic, 133-134, 148, 150, 213, 232; censorship, 118, 129; doctrine of, 71, 76, 82

Pearson, Carlton D'Metrius: approach to scripture, 124-126; "Christ Universal Temple Leader Stepping Down" article, 228, 230n chronology of, ix-xii; 3, marriage of, 60; mayoral race of, 87-89; personality and speaking style of, 21,40; religious background of, 47, 50; speaking at Byron Davis' funeral, 189

Pentecostal, 2; Pentecostal blackness, 50

photographs: Barack Obama Campaign, *111*; Higher D members with actress, Lisa Bonet, *106*; Higher D sanctuary, *105*; members of the elite High D choir, *107*; Musician at Higher D, *113*

prophecy, 1; prophets, 1; prophetic utterance, 2

Pearson, Gina Marie (nee Gauthier) (wife), ix, xi; final service, 180; "First Lady", 61; marriage of, 60; Pastor Carlton's sermons, 61; "The Pastor and First Lady

of Higher Dimensions", *112*

Pearson, Julian D'Metrius (son), ix, 61; the final service, 180

Pearson, Lillie Ruth (nee Johnson) (mother), ix, 65; "Mom & Dad" Pearson, *103*; style of, 66

Pearson, Majeste' Amor (daughter), x; 61; final service, 180

Reed, Teresa L.: arrival at Higher Dimensions, 45; ministry service of, 24, 169; ministry work at Trinity, 182; personal background of, 18, 23-24, 45-46, 69-70,72-75, 92-93, 157-160; "Together in the House of the Lord", *110*

Reed, Teresa "Closing Reflection", 240-242

repentance, 165

Robert, Morgan, 1

scriptures: Eph. 3:20, 41; Pslm. 121, 19; Pslm. 139:8, 91; II Cor. 5:19, 71, 2 Tim. 2:17, 151

September 11th Terrorist Attacks, 116-117

Smith, David, 15, 25n, 81, 124, 166, 169, 174, 200, 202, 219, 220, 224; appreciation service for, 166-167; at Azusa, 53, 120; directing recording sessions, 57, 118

S. Memorial Drive, ix, x, xi, 12, 23, 183, 184, 186, 188, 224, 233; final service at, 179; foot-traffic of, 13; last Azusa conference, 118-

119; last Sunday service at,
178
St. Augustine, xiii
Tiansay, Eric, 155n
Titanic, The, 2
Todd, Brenda, 16-18, 25n
Trinity Episcopal Church: choir
        rehearsals at, 183; decrease
        in Higher D supporters
        while at, 186, 190;
        departure from, 208, 211;
        description of, 181;
        services at, 181, 206;
        Jennifer's death at, 186-
        187; ministries at, 182;
        reuniting with the
        estranged at, 187;
        temporary home in, 184,
        186, 190
Tulsa Race Massacre, 212
Tulsa World newspaper, x; Bill
        Sherman's story, 214;
        interview with, 88
Tulsa's Circle Cinema, 230
Tulsa Convention Center: Azusa
        2002, 117
Universalism, 207, 208, 213
unsavory headlines for Christianity,
        232-233
ushers: appearance of, 14
Williams, Jesse, 19, 25n, 166, 191,
        212, 219; background of,
        199-200; appearance of, 20;
        at Azusa, 53; death of,
        221 health decline of, 201-
        203, 219-220

Wright Brothers, The, 1

For more information about future publications
contact:

GarySprings Independent Press, LLC
P.O. Box 691272
Tulsa, Oklahoma 74169-1272

BeneathAHereticsWings@gmail.com

GarySprings
Independent Press, LLC
Tulsa, Oklahoma